weird but true! 2022

NATIONAL GEOGRAPHIC KiDS

Published by Collins
An imprint of HarperCollins Publishers
Westerhill Road
Bishopbriggs
Glasgow G64 2QT
www.harpercollins.co.uk

HarperCollins Publishers
1st Floor, Watermarque Building, Ringsend Road, Dublin 4, Ireland

In association with National Geographic Partners, LLC

NATIONAL GEOGRAPHIC and the Yellow Border Design are trademarks of
the National Geographic Society and used under license.

National Geographic Kids Weird But True & Design are trademarks of
National Geographic Society and used under license.

First published 2021

ISBN 978-0-00-846381-6

10 9 8 7 6 5 4 3 2 1

A catalogue record for this book is available from the British Library

Printed in Italy by Rotolito S.p.A.

If you would like to comment on any aspect of this book, please contact
us at the above address or online.
natgeokidsbooks.co.uk
collins.reference@harpercollins.co.uk

Paper from responsible sources.

NATIONAL
GEOGRAPHIC
KiDS

weird
but
true!

2022

wild & wacky
facts & photos!

Contents

Amazing
EARTH

The word 'VOLCANO' comes from the **ROMAN** name 'VULCAN'. Vulcan was the **ROMAN GOD** OF FIRE.

Read more about volcanoes on page 20.

10 Lightning-quick Facts about Lightning

LIGHTNING STRIKES Earth's surface at around 3 million times a day – that's nearly 44 times every second!

A **BOLT OF LIGHTNING** is about five times hotter than the surface of the Sun but is only about as thick as your thumb.

FULGURITE is a form of glass that is made when lightning strikes sand.

In the right – or rather, the wrong – conditions, helicopters can actually cause **LIGHTNING STRIKES!**

LIGHTNING has been observed on two other planets in the solar system – Jupiter and Saturn.

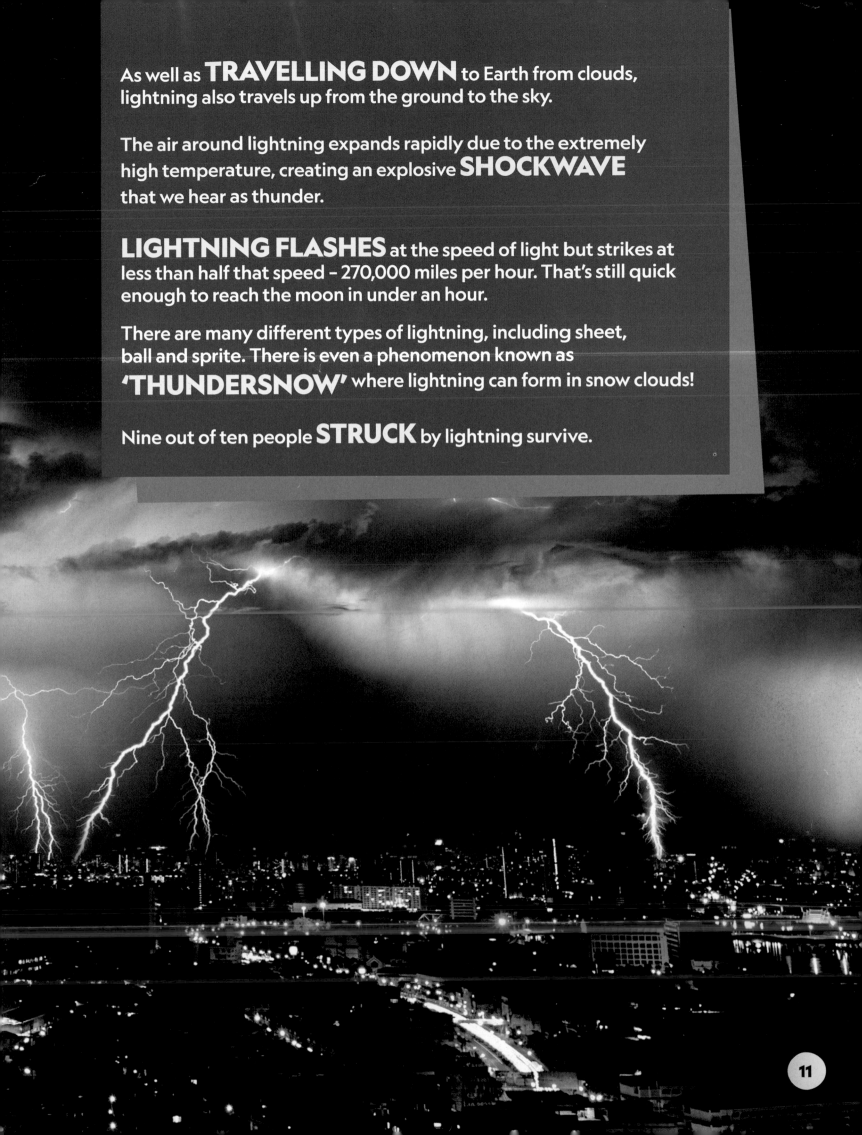

As well as **TRAVELLING DOWN** to Earth from clouds, lightning also travels up from the ground to the sky.

The air around lightning expands rapidly due to the extremely high temperature, creating an explosive **SHOCKWAVE** that we hear as thunder.

LIGHTNING FLASHES at the speed of light but strikes at less than half that speed – 270,000 miles per hour. That's still quick enough to reach the moon in under an hour.

There are many different types of lightning, including sheet, ball and sprite. There is even a phenomenon known as **'THUNDERSNOW'** where lightning can form in snow clouds!

Nine out of ten people **STRUCK** by lightning survive.

See the Wood
FOR THE TREES

DYNAMITE TREE

The sandbox tree is one of the most dangerous trees in the world. It is covered in thorns, is poisonous and has exploding fruit. The sap of the sandbox tree can cause blindness. The fruit of the sandbox tree is poisonous and causes vomiting and diarrhoea. The fruits also explode, sending seeds flying through the air at over 240 kilometres per hour.

THE WOOD-WIDE-WEB

Before trees evolved, the surface of Earth was covered in huge mushrooms. They could reach 8 metres tall, which is about the same height as a house! Mushrooms are vital for trees and forests to grow. Beneath every forest there is a vast hidden network of pale thread-like structures called mycelia – these are all parts of the mushroom or fungus that you don't see. They help to provide trees with the nutrients they need and transport nutrients over long distances.

Totally **WEIRD!**

Over 2,000 years ago, during a battle, a forest was used to crush an advancing Roman army. Literally. Trees in a forest in northern Italy were cut so that just a simple push would cause them to topple like dominoes. When the army marched through the forest, the trees were pushed onto them, leaving only 10 survivors.

TREE IN CUSTODY

A Banyan tree in Pakistan has been under arrest (and held in chains) for over 120 years. The tree was placed under arrest in 1898, when a British Army officer thought he saw the tree moving towards him in a suspicious way. Another Banyan tree, in India (pictured here), is the widest tree in the world – its canopy covers more area than two rugby pitches!

A door to HELL

THIS FIERY HOLE IN THE GROUND IS THE DARVAZA CRATER.

It is a 30-metre-deep pit that has been burning for over 40 years. It is located in a natural gas field in the country of Turkmenistan in central Asia.

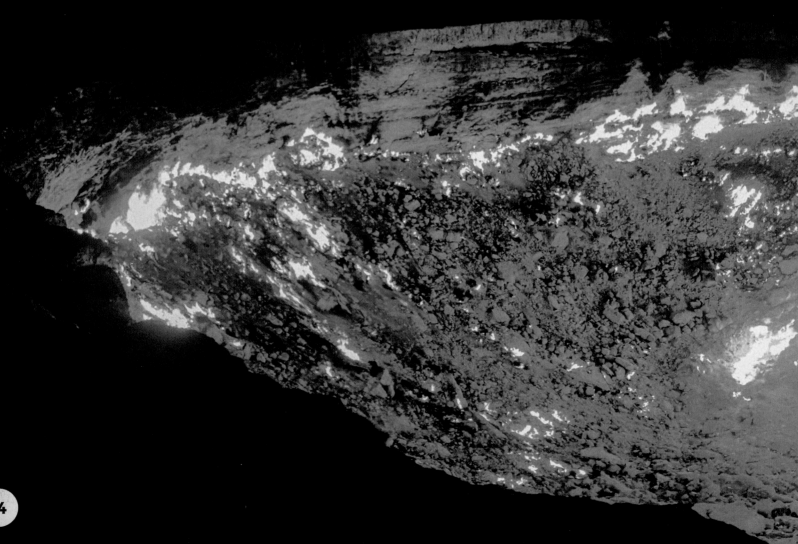

In the early 1970s, an oil rig fell into a hole in a natural gas field. It is thought that geologists decided to sort the problem out by setting the rig on fire. They thought that the natural gas in the hole would burn itself out very quickly. They were wrong!

The crater is known as the 'Door to Hell' and doesn't look like it could have anything living in it. Remarkably, scientists investigated the crater and found a number of extremophile microorganisms living in the depths of the fiery pit—these are creatures that can live in extreme environments.

Scientists study extremophiles because it is amazing that life can be found in such harsh environments. The existence of extremophiles suggests that living beings could be found elsewhere in the solar system—in places we never thought could sustain life.

Did you Know?

You may have noticed that there are a number of countries in the world whose name ends in **'stan'.** There are seven of these countries in total: Pakistan, Uzbekistan, Turkmenistan, Kyrgyzstan, Tajikistan, Kazakhstan and Afghanistan. The 'stan' in each of these names comes from the **Persian word** for 'place of' or 'country'. Uzbekistan is the country of the Uzbek people; Tajikistan is the country of the Tajik people.

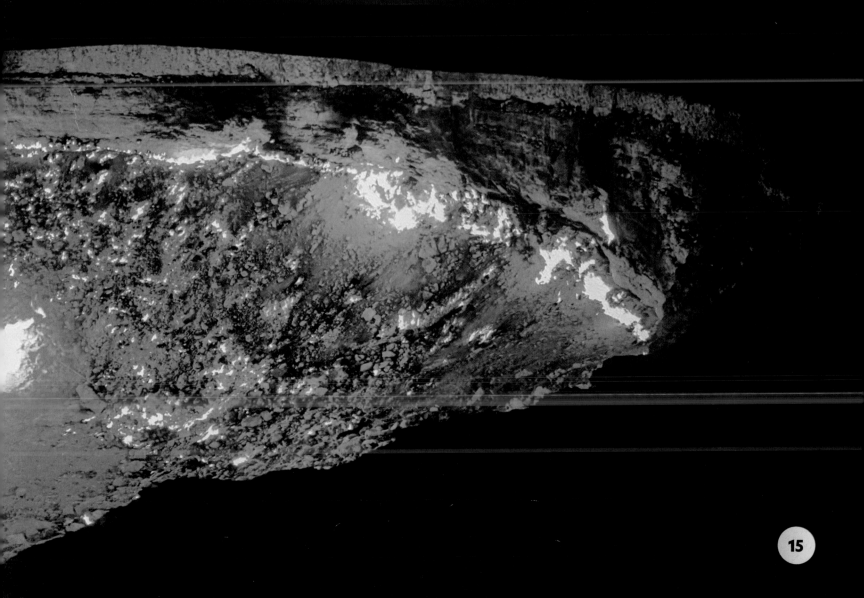

LONG WAY DOWN...

Mount Thor in Canada, named after the Norse god of thunder, features the cliff face with the highest vertical drop in the world. The cliff is over 1 kilometre high (1,250 metres to be exact). It is actually steeper than vertical as it has a 105° overhang.

THERE'S WEIRD IN THEM THERE HILLS

MAGNETIC HILL
THE PHENOMENON THAT DEFIES GRAVITY. PARK YOUR VEHICLE IN THE BOX MARKED WITH PAINT ON THE ROAD & EXPERIANCE THE WONDER!!
- K T N -

... AND ROLL BACK UP?

Some hills in the world seem to defy the laws of gravity. At places such as the appropriately named 'Confusion Hill' in California, 'Magnetic Hill' in Canada or the 'Electric Brae' in Scotland, cars appear to roll up hill!

A LAND OF CHOCOLATE

These cone-shaped hills in the Philippines are known as the Chocolate Hills. They get their name from the plants that live on them, which turn a chocolatey-brown colour in the dry season. Legend has it that they were made by giants, but scientists think that they were made by coral being eroded by rainwater over thousands of years.

CLOSEST TO THE MOON

Standing on top of Mount Everest, you'd be forgiven for thinking that you were on top of the world. And you would be higher than nearly everyone, but not people who had climbed to the summit of Mount Chimborazo, a volcanic mountain in Ecuador. This is because Earth is not a perfect sphere – it bulges out in the middle, meaning that people on the summit of Mount Chimborazo are actually closer to the Moon than the frostbitten climbers on Everest!

17

STRANGE ROCKS

Fairy Chimneys

A hoodoo is a natural rock formation that looks like someone has balanced a large boulder on top of a spire of rock. Cappadocia in Turkey is home to some of these formations (also known as 'fairy chimneys'). They were created from volcanic deposits that were then sculpted by wind and water erosion to create the peculiar stacks we see today.

Home in the Ground

In Matmata, Southern Tunisia, some homes are literally holes in the ground. These are called Troglodyte houses. A hotel in Matmata featured in the Star Wars movies as part of the planet Tatooine.

Hairy Volcanoes

An eruption of the Kilauea volcano in Hawaii created golden strands of what looked like hair. The strands were glass, made by the lava, and were thin and dangerously sharp. The volcanic glass is called 'Pele's Hair' after the Hawaiian goddess of volcanoes.

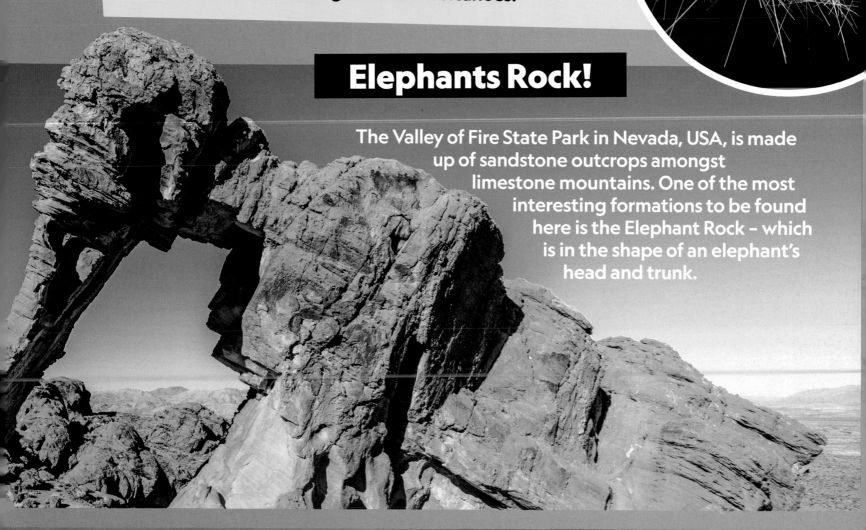

Elephants Rock!

The Valley of Fire State Park in Nevada, USA, is made up of sandstone outcrops amongst limestone mountains. One of the most interesting formations to be found here is the Elephant Rock – which is in the shape of an elephant's head and trunk.

Baikal Zen

Baikal Zen is a strange phenomenon. It occurs when a rock freezes to an icy surface. Over time, wind erodes or the Sun melts the ice below leaving the rock perched on a pedestal.

RING OF FIRE

On Thin Ground

The top layer of our planet – the crust – is very thin: it ranges in depth of between 5 and 70 kilometres. The thin crust is split into massive plates that sit on top of Earth's mantle – hot, viscous molten rock and metal over 2,900 kilometres thick.

Fire at the Edge of the Pacific Ocean

There are around 1,500 active volcanoes on Earth (not counting the volcanoes under the sea). Many of these are around the Pacific Ring of Fire – a 40,000-kilometre chain of volcanoes. This area is also responsible for 90% of the world's earthquakes.

Totally WEIRD!

The deepest volcanic eruption took place at 4,500 metres below sea level. It was discovered in a trough next to the Mariana Trench.

Supervolcano

Yellowstone National Park in the USA hides a secret. There is a massive volcano, called a supervolcano, that sits just beneath it. Eruptions from supervolcanoes are rare: the most recent was 27,000 years ago when a supervolcano named Taupo erupted in New Zealand.

Surprise Volcano

Some volcanoes grow quickly. In 1943, in a field in Mexico, a crack in the ground appeared and lava started to pour out. Within a day, the Parícutin volcano was 50 metres tall. That's the height of the Arc de Triomphe in Paris! Within a week, the volcano was taller than Big Ben. Within a year it was well over 300 metres tall – nearly as tall as the Empire State Building.

Mashed Together

All of the continents used to be mashed together into one giant landmass called Pangea. Over millions of years, the land separated into the continents as they are today. Look at a map of the world and you will see that the continents of Africa and South America look a little like two separated jigsaw puzzle pieces.

before

after

A Humungous FUNGUS

The **LARGEST LIVING ANIMAL** in the history of the world is the **BLUE WHALE**. Growing to lengths of over 30 metres (longer than some passenger jets), they spend their lives eating tiny sea creatures called krill. A single whale can eat 40 million krill every day.

But the **LARGEST LIVING ORGANISM** that we have discovered is actually a **MUSHROOM**.

A single **HONEY MUSHROOM** was discovered in the hills of **MICHIGAN** in 1992 that was reported in 2018 to cover 70 hectares – around the same area as Greenwich Park in London. Scientists estimate that it is over **2,500 YEARS OLD!**

Honey mushrooms feed on trees and plant matter. A team investigating a dying patch of forest in **OREGON** found one **GIGANTIC MUSHROOM** was to blame. It turned out to be the largest living organism on Earth and measured at **9.6 SQUARE KILOMETRES.** That's about 20 times the size of Vatican City! It could also be one of the **OLDEST ORGANISMS EVER.** It is at least 1,900 years old and could be as old as 8,650!

Step back in
TIME

The **PYRAMID OF KHUFU** at **GIZA** is so **BIG** it **WEIGHS** as much as **16** EMPIRE STATE BUILDINGS.

Explore more on pyramids on page 28.

On Your Marks, Get Set... To Be Late!

In 1908, some Russian Olympic competitors were 12 days late to the games in London as they were not used to using the Gregorian calendar yet (they were using the Julian calendar —the one made by Julius Caesar).

From Russia, With Weird

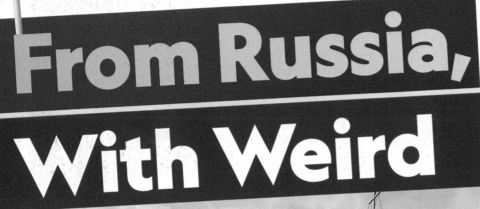

For Ivan's Eyes Only

Legend says that in the 16th century, Ivan the Terrible ordered the architect who designed the amazing St Basil's Cathedral in Red Square, Moscow, to be blinded! It is said he did it so that nothing so beautiful could ever be designed again.

The Tsar With the Dragon Tattoo

Tsar Nicholas II had a tattoo of a dragon on his right forearm, which he got on a visit to Nagasaki in Japan in 1891. The procedure lasted 7 hours. During the same trip an attempt was made on his life.

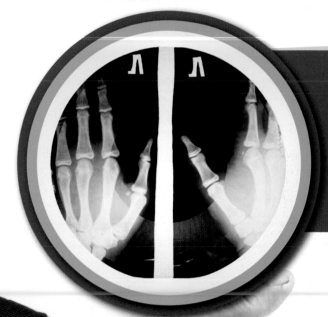

Bone Music

In the 1950s, popular music from the US and Britain was not allowed in Russia. To get around this ban, people pressed records in secret on to old X-rays of people's chests, legs, arms and heads!

World War II is over, right?

Russia and Japan are technically still at war with each other from World War II. They did not sign a peace treaty at the end of the war, though they did stop fighting, as there was an argument about who owns the islands of the archipelago between them in the eastern Pacific, called the Kuril Islands by the Russians and Chishima Islands by the Japanese.

PYRAMIDS
EVERYWHERE!

PYRAMIDS OF GIZA

The pyramids at **Giza,** in **Egypt,** are by far the most famous in the world. The three main pyramids (the tallest, for **Pharaoh Khufu,** the second tallest for **Pharaoh Khafre,** and the smallest for **Pharaoh Menkaure**) were all built – we think – in a **60**-year period around 4,500 years ago. Over **100** pyramids have been discovered in **Egypt** so far.

The word '**pyramid**' is not an **Egyptian** word. It comes from the **Greek** word for a wheat cake because, when the Greeks first saw these amazing structures (which, for 4,000 years, were the tallest things in the world built by people) on the banks of the Nile river, the shape reminded them of the pointy cakes *pyramis,* that they made. The **Egyptians** themselves called the pyramids 'mer', which means 'place of ascendance'.

THE GODS OF ANCIENT EGYPT

The Ancient Egyptians believed in many different gods. There were over **2,000** of them! There were gods of the sun (**Ra** – a hawk-headed god, who was eaten every night by **Nut,** the goddess of the sky, the stars and the universe), the moon (**Khonsu** – responsible for time), and war (**Horus** – who had a falcon's head and a human body). There was even a goddess, **Ammit,** who was part hippo, part lion and part crocodile and who was known as '**The Devourer of the Dead**'.

THE 'MOOSE' THAT SURVIVED A SHOOTING

In 1912, Theodore Roosevelt—former President of the United States (1901–1909) and a candidate for the upcoming Presidency—was about to give a speech when someone walked up to him and shot him in the chest. A matter of minutes later, Mr Roosevelt said:

'Friends, I shall ask you to be as quiet as possible. I don't know whether you fully understand that I have just been shot; but it takes more than that to kill a Bull Moose. But fortunately, I had my manuscript, so you see I was going to make a long speech, and there is a bullet—there is where the bullet went through—and it probably saved me from it going into my heart. The bullet is in me now, so that I cannot make a very long speech, but I will try my best.'

Theodore Roosevelt was tough—and lucky. His speech was 50 pages long and he had folded it up in his inside pocket, which had almost stopped the bullet. Thankfully, Roosevelt survived, but he didn't win the election.

A HOST OF HOAXES

LEFTY LAUGHS

A number of April Fools' pranks have been directed at left-handed people. In 1996, adverts showed a left-handed chocolate bar; in 1997, a left-handed laptop; in 1998 a left-handed burger. More recently, people have been pranked with left-handed mobile phones, pizzas, golf balls, pint glasses, toilet paper and even dogs!

WASHING OF THE LIONS

It was reported in a newspaper that on 1 April 1698, people could go to the Tower of London moat to watch a group of lions being washed. This was a total and utter lie, but the prank has become an April Fools' day tradition amongst Londoners ever since!

SUNNY, FUNNY SANS SERIFFE

On April Fools' Day in 1977, newspaper readers in Britain were invited to apply for a position at the University of San Seriffe to study whether it was possible to extract energy from moon-beams. Lots of people applied but the university did not exist!

PAPER TOWNS

You could find a 'paper town' on a map, but nowhere else. Before the digital age, cartographers (map-makers) would put fake towns onto maps so they could tell if someone else had copied their work.

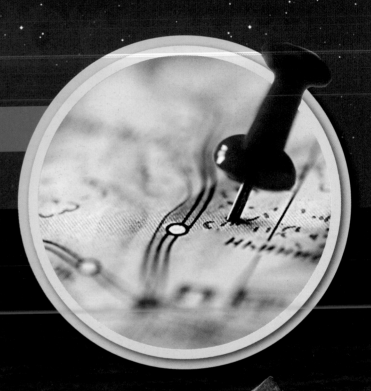

CHOPPING DOWN THE OLDEST TREE

In 2014, it was reported that the world's oldest tree had been cut down in the Amazon Rainforest. It wasn't true, but lots of people got very angry about it. However, in 1964, by accident a science graduate caused the world's oldest tree (a bristlecone pine called Prometheus that was around 5,000 years old) to be cut down as part of a study.

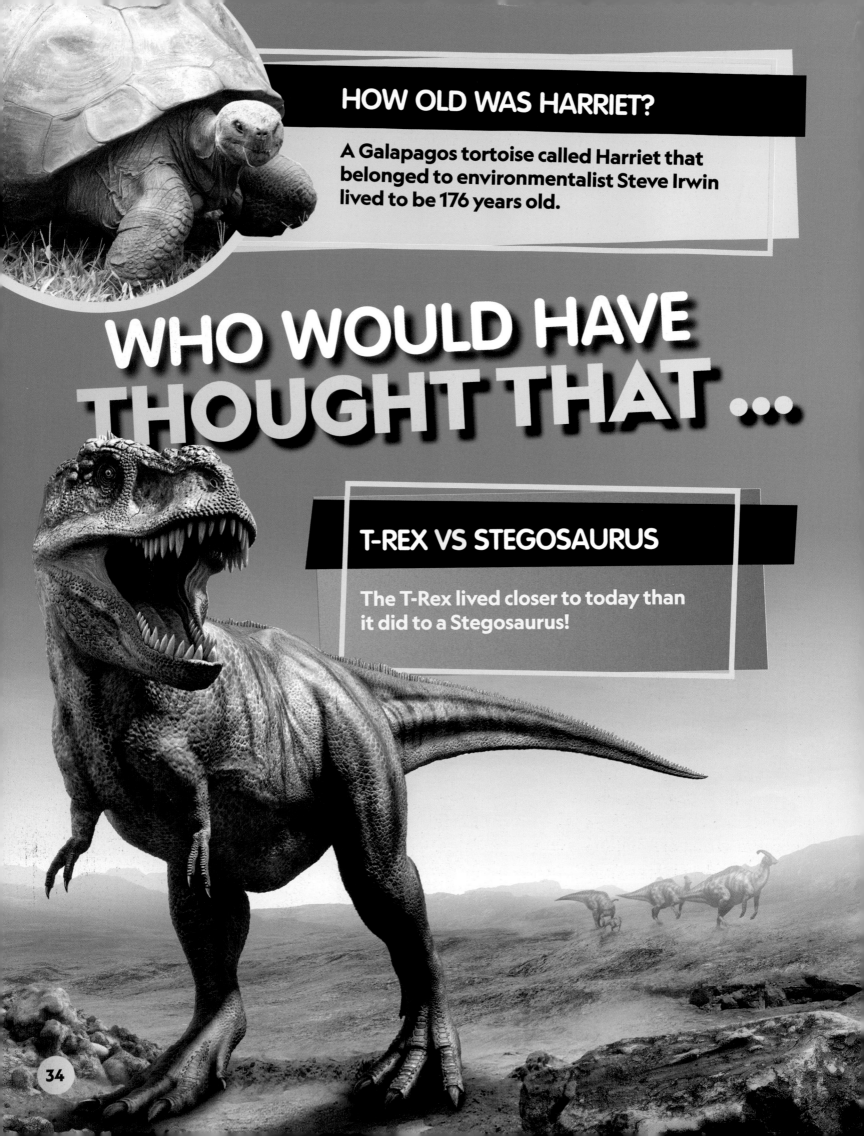

HOW OLD WAS HARRIET?

A Galapagos tortoise called Harriet that belonged to environmentalist Steve Irwin lived to be 176 years old.

WHO WOULD HAVE THOUGHT THAT ...

T-REX VS STEGOSAURUS

The T-Rex lived closer to today than it did to a Stegosaurus!

THE QUEEN OF EGYPT VS THE MOON LANDINGS

Queen Cleopatra of Egypt lived closer to the time of the Moon landings than she did to the building of the first pyramids at Giza. The pyramids were built 2550 BC–2490 BC and Cleopatra died in 30 BC.

THE CAR THAT STARTED AND ENDED THE WAR

The car that Archduke Franz Ferdinand was in when he was assassinated – which caused the start of World War I – had a licence plate that had the date of the end of the war on it: A111 1118 – 11 November 1918.

NO SCHOOL LIKE THE OLD SCHOOL

Teaching began in Oxford by 1096 and developed rapidly from around 1167; so the university, in some form, existed more than 300 years before the historic Incan city of Machu Picchu was built!

THE PIG WAR AND OTHER
BIZARRE BATTLES

HOG OF WAR

In **1859,** a pig stealing potatoes from a farm triggered a war between the **United States** and **the United Kingdom.**

SHORT BUT NOT SWEET

The shortest war in history took place in 1896 between **the United Kingdom** and **Zanzibar**. It only lasted **38** minutes.

THE DOG OF WAR

Greece and **Bulgaria** went to war – briefly – in **1925** because a soldier had run after his dog which had strayed into enemy territory.

INFIGHTING AUSTRIANS

In **1788,** a part of the **Austrian** army got confused and started fighting itself, leading to the loss of the town they were defending to their real enemy, Turkey.

DON'T INSULT OUR KING

In **1883,** a village in **Spain** declared war on **France** after the Spanish king was mocked in Paris. It lasted for nearly **100** years, but nobody was killed.

THE VERY LONG WAR

A war between the **Netherlands** and the **Scilly Isles** (located south of the United Kingdom) lasted so long that the two sides forgot they were at war. It lasted **335** years. The war started in **1651** but despite being finished, the peace treaty to end it wasn't signed until **1986**.

Marvels of
THE
MAYANS

Comalcalco Temple I found in Tabasco, Mexico.

El Castillo, Mexico

THE MAYAN CIVILISATION BEGAN AROUND 4,000 YEARS AGO AND ALTHOUGH THEIR CITIES HAVE LONG SINCE BEEN ABANDONED, MAYAN PEOPLE STILL LIVE IN GUATEMALA, MEXICO AND OTHER LATIN AMERICAN COUNTRIES.

Mayans were excellent at astronomy, creating weapons, ball games and building pyramids and cities.

Mayans built a massive city—only discovered in 2020—about 3,000 years ago in what is now the Mexican state of Tabasco.

Mayans (and other cultures from Latin America, including the Aztecs, the Incans, the Olmecs and the Toltecs) built pyramids. Most of these were stepped pyramids, meaning that the sides of the pyramids were not smooth. Chichen Itza in Mexico is home to El Castillo, a huge Mayan pyramid that was built so that during equinoxes (the days of the year that have equal sunlight and darkness) a shadow, known as 'the serpent' creeps down the staircase of the pyramid and joins up with a carved snake's head.

Mayans did not have iron or steel, but used obsidian (below) to make weapons, tools and jewellery. Obsidian is a volcanic rock—it is sharp but brittle, which means it can shatter easily. Obsidian is made in volcanoes and is usually black in colour. One place—known as Cerro de las Navajas—the Hill of Knives—produced green obsidian, which was highly prized by Mayans.

Incredible
CREATURES

FLAMINGOS are born **WHITE** and with a **STRAIGHT BILL.** As they get **OLDER,** the **BILL** begins to **CURVE DOWN.**

Fly over to page 46 for more brilliant bird facts.

Cockatoo
DANCE-OFF

COCKATOOS are the **ONLY ANIMAL** that we know of that **MAKE THEIR OWN MUSICAL INSTRUMENTS.**

WILD WHACKERS!

In the wild, the **PALM COCKATOO** makes **drumsticks** out of **twigs** and **seed pods.** It uses these to **beat a rhythm** on tree trunks. Each cockatoo has its own rhythm. Male cockatoos use their **drumming patterns** to attract a mate.

AT HOME...

When raised as **pets,** cockatoos form very **strong bonds** with their owners and can get **depressed** – pulling out their own feathers or **destroying furniture** – if they don't get the **attention** they need!

Totally **WEIRD!**

After a video of a dancing pet cockatoo named Snowball went viral on the internet, scientists studied it and found that the bird bobbed its head, shuffled its feet, and flapped its wings in time with different types of music. It made up 14 dance moves of its own. Its favourite moves were a 'side-to-side' step and head-banging!

BEETLE BUM BOMBS

Bombardier beetles shoot out a boiling hot mix of chemicals from their bums when threatened.

DISGUSTING DEFENCES

WARNING – I'M NOT TIRED!

If you see a hippo yawning, don't think that it is sleepy: hippos yawn to show off their huge mouths and teeth as a warning.

DANGER SIGNS!

Monarch butterflies are beautifully coloured – but for a very good reason. It is to warn any predators against eating them. Monarch butterflies are full of toxins. They get this from eating milkweed, which is poisonous to predators.

SHOCKING FISH

Electric eels have special organs that generate electricity – over 800 volts – providing enough shocking power to knock a horse off its feet!

DON'T MIND ME!

Possums have a strange defence against predators; they 'play dead' by going into a deep sleep and stinking like a rotting corpse.

BLOODSHOT EYES

The horned lizard shoots blood out of its eyes to defend itself against predators.

A FLOCK of FACTS

THE PHILIPPINE EAGLE is one of the largest eagles in the world. It snacks on monkeys, squirrels, pigs and even dogs!

OILBIRDS are a lot like bats. They sleep during the day, roost in caves and use echolocation (listening to the echoes made from their squawks) to find their way around.

SWIFTS spend most of their lives flying. Young swifts can spend four years in the air without ever landing once!

OSTRICHES have the biggest eyes of any animal that lives on land. An ostrich's eye is bigger than its brain!

There are more plastic **FLAMINGOS** in the USA than there are real ones!

A **SWORD-BILLED HUMMINGBIRD'S** beak is 10 centimetres long. That's longer than its whole body (excluding the tail)!

KIWIS are the only birds that have nostrils at the end of their beaks. Kiwis are flightless birds, so having nostrils at the tip of their bills makes finding food in the undergrowth easier.

THE HORNED SCREAMER, as well as having an odd name, grows a thin white horn in the middle of its forehead! Scientists believe the horn is for ornamental purposes.

OUR
mutual
FRIENDS

THE WASP FIG FACTORY

Without wasps we wouldn't have figs. Figs are not a fruit, but a pod of tiny flowers that depend on wasps to survive and reproduce. There are around 750 types of fig and each has a species of wasp that lays its eggs inside the figs.

POLLINATION POWER

Birds, bees and other insects collect pollen from flowers as they drink the sugary nectar produced by the plants. They then spread the pollen to other plants. Some researchers believe over 300,000 species of plant reproduce in this way.

THORN DEFENDERS

Bullhorn acacia trees that grow in Central America have evolved hollow thorns that sprout leaf stems with a nectary at the base. One species of ant lives inside the thorns and drinks the nectar. The ants return the favour by defending the trees from any attackers.

THE FLOWERS ARE LISTENING

Scientists have discovered that flowers – the evening primrose to be exact – listen out for the sounds of bees nearby. Don't bother singing to them though: the flowers only respond to the buzzing sounds made by bees. When they hear the buzz, they produce sweeter nectar, and in greater amounts!

GRUB'S UP!

When large blue butterflies are caterpillars, they give off a smell that attracts a particular species of ant. The smell tricks the ants into thinking that the caterpillar is a baby ant. The ants adopt the caterpillars and take them back to their nest... where the caterpillars feast on baby ant grubs!

SHRIMPY CLEAN

Pederson shrimps set up cleaning stations in coral reefs. Fish arrive at the cleaning station and stay still. They then signal (by changing colour) that they are ready to be cleaned. The shrimp get to work, eating up harmful parasites and removing damaged bits of the fish to help the fish heal.

PROTECT THE
PANGOLINS

Pangolins are the only mammals on the planet that are fully covered in scales! They are native to India, China, southeast Asia and parts of Africa.

When threatened, pangolins roll into a ball—their scales form a shield that even the teeth and claws of lions, tigers and leopards often can't get through. But although pangolins seem pretty well protected already, they are endangered. Weirdly, their scales are the reason why pangolins need to be protected—from humans.

Some people think that the scales of a pangolin (which are made from the same stuff as our hair and fingernails, a substance called keratin) can be used to make medicine. This belief means that pangolins are illegally hunted and traded, threatening their survival.

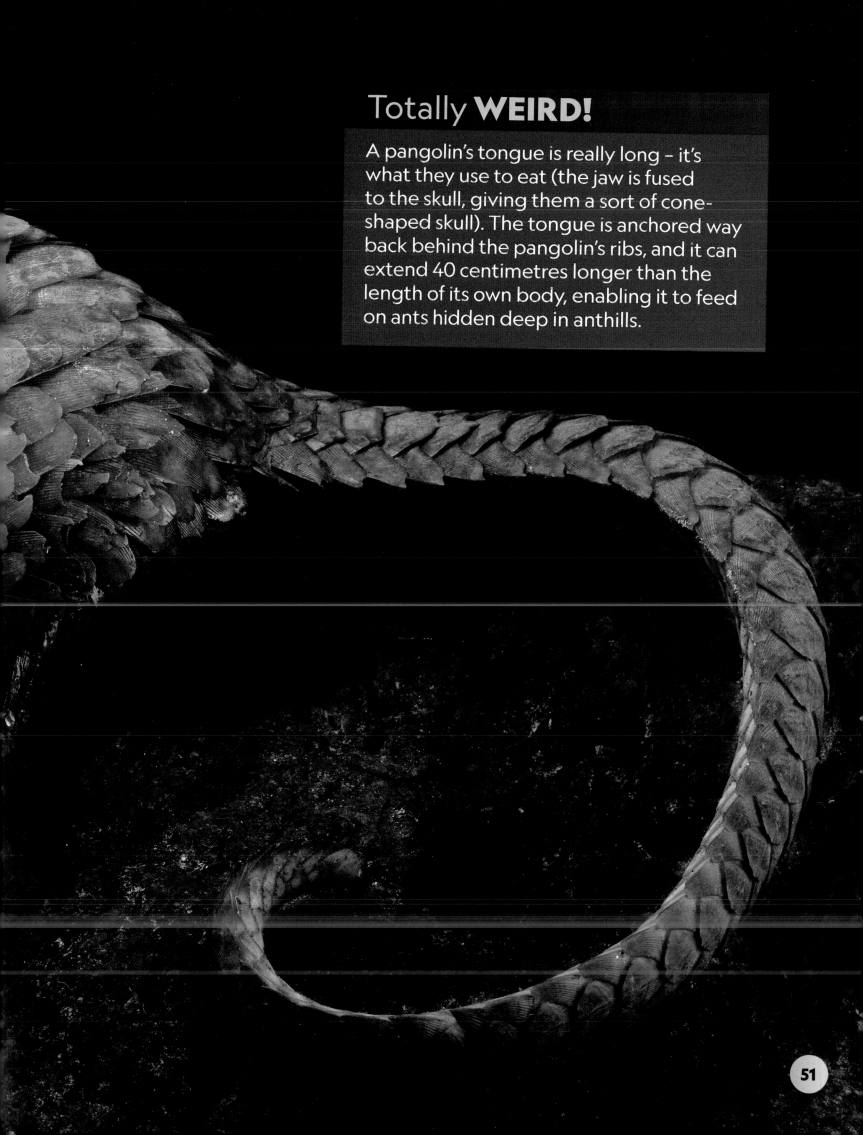

Totally **WEIRD!**

A pangolin's tongue is really long – it's what they use to eat (the jaw is fused to the skull, giving them a sort of cone-shaped skull). The tongue is anchored way back behind the pangolin's ribs, and it can extend 40 centimetres longer than the length of its own body, enabling it to feed on ants hidden deep in anthills.

A helping h~~hand~~ PAW!

The first school to train guide dogs was set up in New Jersey, USA, in 1929 by Morris Frank and his German shepherd, Buddy. However, dogs aren't the only helpful animals out there...

I SMELL A RAT!

African giant pouched rats have been trained to sniff out landmines and have helped to clear thousands of mines from Tanzania, Mozambique, **Angola,** and Cambodia.

COME FLY WITH ME

In 2018, there were over 75,000 requests for **support animals** to be brought on to flights in the USA. Animals that have helped anxious owners on flights include turkeys, ducks and even **miniature horses.** Assistance **peacocks** and support hamsters were both **turned away** though!

UNDERWATER HELPERS

Bottlenose dolphins have been used to search for underwater mines for over **50 years.** Their high levels of intelligence, super underwater vision and **sonar** help them detect the **explosives.**

HUNTING FOR TRUFFLES

Pigs are used to sniff out **expensive,** edible fungi called truffles. Even if the truffles are buried underground, the pig's excellent sense of **smell** can locate them.

GONE FISHING

In **China** and Japan, **cormorants** have been used for centuries to help people catch fish.

These creatures really suck... BLOOD!

DRACULA'S FAVOURITE?

Vampire bats have got a reputation for drinking human blood. And sometimes they do. There are three species of bat that only drink blood. One of them—the hairy-legged vampire bat—has been found to have human blood in their diet too!

DRINK UP!

It would take over a million mosquitoes to entirely drain a human being of all their blood. Only female mosquitoes actually drink blood and it's their saliva that reacts with your skin and causes the itchy bump.

LOOOOONG LEECHES

The largest bloodsucking leech in the world lives in the Amazon and can grow up to 45 centimetres long. There is a longer leech – the Kinabalu leech, that can grow up to 50 centimetres long. But don't worry – the Kinabalu only feeds on earthworms in Borneo.

FLEA BITTEN

You might think that fleas are a problem for dogs. And they are. But fleas were also responsible for carrying the bubonic plague (they hitched a ride on rats), which resulted in the death of about 20 million people in Europe, or 5% of all the people in the world at that time.

BLOOD BUDDIES

Oxpeckers are native to Africa. They like to feast on ticks and insects they find on other beasts such as giraffes, buffalos and zebras. They are also known to peck at animal wounds to feed on blood and tissue.

HIDE AND SEEK

comes naturally to some...

SLOW AND MOULDY WINS THE RACE

Sloths have gardens of green algae that grow on their backs. It helps to keep the sloths camouflaged in the treetops, where they spend most of their days slowly eating leaves. Entire ecosystems exist in the green gunk that grows on sloths.

BLENDYPUS

Octopuses, squid and cuttlefish are all cephalopods, which means head-foot in Greek. They all have remarkable abilities to change colour to blend in with their surroundings.

HIDDEN PEARLFISH

Sea cucumbers taste disgusting, so they are generally left alone. They also breathe through their bum and pearlfish (sometimes more than one of them) take advantage of this by quickly swimming in there to hide from predators.

DECEPTIVE DISGUISE

The scarlet king snake is not venomous, but its brightly striped body looks almost identical to the pattern of the coral snake. And coral snakes most definitely are venomous!

NOTHING TO 'SEA' HERE

The leafy sea dragon looks almost exactly like a strand of seaweed floating along the ocean currents in the waters around Australia. It is a brilliant way of hiding in plain sight.

BRILLIANTLY BLACK

Black birds?

There are around 26 billion chickens in the world. In other words, for every one human, there are three chickens. One breed of chicken – the Ayam cemani – is perhaps the most striking type of chicken on the planet. Its feathers, beak, comb and tongue are all blue-black in colour. Even its skin, bones and internal organs are black!

Raccoons

Raccoons are born blind and deaf but quickly develop into skilful foragers. In the wild, raccoons hunt frogs, mice and insects, as well as munching on fruit and plants. In urban areas they will eat anything they can get their hands on, from sweets to pizza! Raccoons need to eat a lot to build up body fat in preparation for sleeping through the winter.

Tapirs

Malayan tapirs' two-tone colouring helps them to camouflage in their rainforest surroundings.

WONDERFULLY WHITE

Dalmatians

Dalmatians are iconic pooches. They are well known for their bright white coats, peppered with black spots. However, dalmatian puppies are born with spots only on their skin – spots don't appear on their fur until they are around 10 days old.

White peaocks

White peacocks are a mutated species of the well-known blue peacock – their white colour is because of a missing pigment.

Giant leopard moths

The giant leopard moth (also called the eyed tiger moth) gets its name from its black ring-and-dot markings.

Super science and TECHNOLOGY

More than **HALF** of the **WORLD'S** **GOOGLE SEARCHES** take place on a **MOBILE DEVICE.**

Discover more internet facts on page 64.

Storm in a Teacup

Teabags were invented by accident! Thomas Sullivan, a tea seller, started giving away samples in little silk bags. These proved to be more popular than loose tea and the teabag was born.

Just the Fax, Please

The fax machine was invented in 1843 and by 1865 was being used to send messages between Paris and Lyon in France (a distance of over 450 kilometres). The telephone wouldn't be invented for another 11 years!

Inventions

Dog and Cat Translators

Believe it or not, people have actually claimed to have invented apps and machines that can translate the woof of a dog or the meow of a cat into human language.

Artificial Heart Invented

Paul Winchell, who famously provided the voice for Tigger in Disney's Winnie-the-Pooh animations, was an inventor who developed the world's first artificial heart!

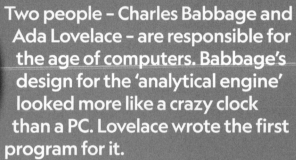

The Difference Engine

Two people – Charles Babbage and Ada Lovelace – are responsible for the age of computers. Babbage's design for the 'analytical engine' looked more like a crazy clock than a PC. Lovelace wrote the first program for it.

Whoopee Rome

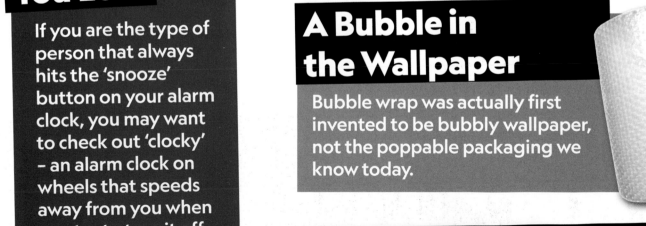

Roman emperor Elagabalus was an odd character. During crazy parties, he would place bags of air under his guests, which made the famous raspberry sound. He also let lions, leopards and bears into the bedrooms of his guests at night – as pranks!

You Snooze, You Lose

If you are the type of person that always hits the 'snooze' button on your alarm clock, you may want to check out 'clocky' – an alarm clock on wheels that speeds away from you when you try to turn it off.

A Bubble in the Wallpaper

Bubble wrap was actually first invented to be bubbly wallpaper, not the poppable packaging we know today.

100 Degrees Freezing

Although we now know that 100°C is the temperature at which water boils, Anders Celsius, who developed the temperature system, originally thought that 100 should be the temperature that water froze at and 0 should be the temperature it boiled at.

Apps Everywhere

Between Apple and Google's stores, there are nearly **5 million** mobile apps to choose from!

WORLD WIDE WEB

Totally WEIRD!

There are over 30 billion devices connected to the internet. That's around four for every human on Earth.

COFFEE CAM

The first webcam was used to monitor a coffee maker at **Cambridge University** so the workers in the computer lab could avoid a trip to an empty pot.

Search Energy

A Google search uses as much energy as your body burns in **10 seconds**. With over **3.5 billion** searches per day, that's a lot of energy being used!

Spam before the Internet

The internet was created in **1989** by Tim Berners-Lee, but spam email had already been around for over **10 years** by then. The first spam email was sent by a salesman to **600 people** in **1978**.

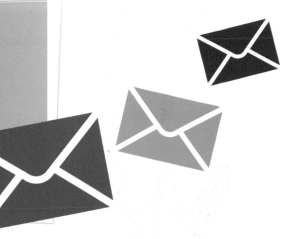

Cat Mail

Years before Google released Gmail, the creators of a **lasagne-loving cartoon cat** called **Garfield** offered 'g-mail' as a webmail service to fans!

YouTube

More than **1 billion hours** of videos are viewed every day on YouTube. The site also has over **2 billion monthly users**!

YOU, Robot

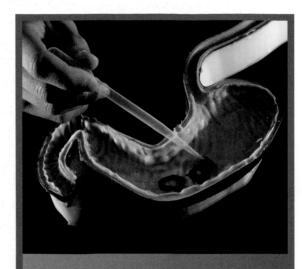

EAT ME!

Have you ever eaten a robot? Scientists are developing an 'origami robot' that can be swallowed and will unfold inside us to safely find things we swallow – like a battery – or even patch an internal wound.

ROBOTIC RECEPTION

A hotel in Japan was once staffed by more robots than humans. However, some of the robots ultimately made more work for their human colleagues resulting in robots being 'fired', including two velociraptors.

ANIME ROBOT MECH

Kuratas is the type of robot you might expect to see in a Sci-Fi movie – it's a giant robot suit that has machine guns that fire ball bearings and rocket launchers that fire plastic rockets filled with compressed water or fireworks!

I, CYBORG

Kevin Warwick, a professor of cybernetics at the University of Reading, UK, turned himself into a cyborg – a mix of human and robot. In 1998, he had a computer chip implanted in his body and in 2002 he had more electronics added so that he could control robot arms remotely.

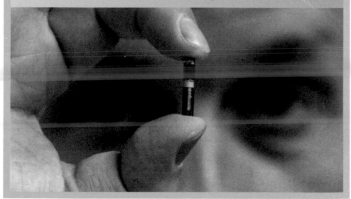

ROCK, PAPER, ROBOT

The *Janken* robot, designed to play 'rock, paper, scissors', will always win against a human opponent– because the robot cheats! *Janken* looks for clues in the human's hand as it makes a shape.

Cloning

Genetics

and

Medical Weirdness

CHARLES GUTHRIE

This brilliant scientist lost out on a **Nobel Prize** because the credit for his research into **vascular surgery**, which included grafting a dog's head onto another dog's body in **1908**, went to his collaborator.

HWANG WOO SUK

This **scientist** created the first **cloned dog** in 2005. More recently he has been trying to clone a woolly mammoth using tissue found in Russia.

BLUE EYES

People with **blue eyes** share one **common ancestor** who lived between **6,000** and **10,000** years ago.

URCHIN

German scientist Hans Driesch cloned a **sea urchin** way back in 1885!

DARK MATTER IN YOUR GUTS

Much of the stuff that lives in your **gut** is called **'Biological Dark Matter'** because it hasn't been biologically **classified**. Scientists have no idea what it is!

THE CLONE MORES

Although Dolly the sheep was the **first mammal** to be **cloned**, there have been many others, including dogs, cats, camels, deer, cows, goats, pigs, rabbits, horses and wolves!

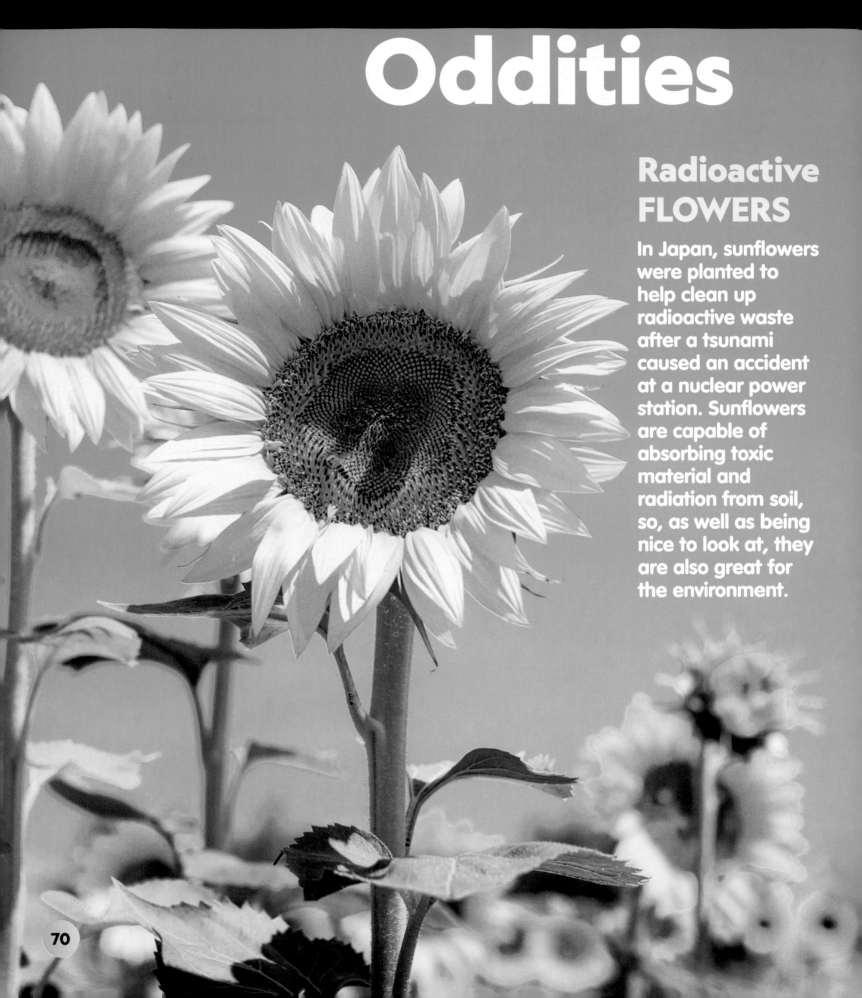

ENVIRONMENTAL
Oddities

Radioactive FLOWERS

In Japan, sunflowers were planted to help clean up radioactive waste after a tsunami caused an accident at a nuclear power station. Sunflowers are capable of absorbing toxic material and radiation from soil, so, as well as being nice to look at, they are also great for the environment.

Pause for Pandemic

The global Covid-19 pandemic had a positive impact on the environment. In 2020, because countries were in lockdown, emissions fell by 7%. The United Kingdom's carbon emissions fell by 13% – the greatest drop since the end of World War II.

STOP the Cows from BURPING

Cows burp methane – a gas that contributes to global warming. Feeding a type of seaweed to cows has been shown to reduce the amount of methane they produce. The problem is that there are around 1.5 billion cows in the world and not enough seaweed to go around.

Window Power

Solar cells turn sunlight into electricity. While these are not new, scientists are developing transparent solar cells so one day soon your windows could be generating power!

71

GREEN the SAHARA

THE GREAT GREEN WALL is an ambitious project in Africa that is trying to stop the Sahara – the largest hot desert in the world – from getting any bigger. When complete, the project will see trees and vegetation planted in a strip right across the continent – around 8,000 kilometres in length. It will end up being the largest living structure on the planet – three times the size of the Great Barrier Reef off the eastern coast of Australia.

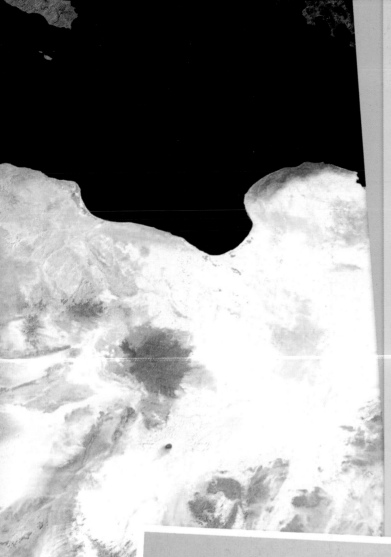

Climate change is causing desertification—the transformation of farmland into dusty desert. Over 500 million people live in the drylands zone, which crosses through Burkina Faso, Djibouti, Eritrea, Ethiopia, Mali, Mauritania, Niger, Nigeria, Senegal, Sudan and Chad. While it started out as a tree-planting project, the Great Green Wall has grown to combat soil erosion, create jobs and keep people from migrating away from their home countries.

Over the past 100 years, the Sahara has been estimated to have grown by 10% in size. In the countries where the desert is advancing, the Green Wall will help to keep the Sahara from getting any bigger.

In China, the Green Great Wall (properly called the Three-North Shelter Forest Program) started to be planted in the late 1970s and won't be completed until 2050. It is a massive forest-planting project in the north of the country that is designed to stop the Gobi desert from expanding.

People planting trees for the Great Green Wall Project on the outskirts of Khartoum, Sudan.

GAMING

GOOD GAMER

Playing video games could be good for you. Scientific studies have shown that video games are linked to an increase in the size of parts of your brain. They have also shown that they can improve your memory and can reduce the experience of pain!

ENTERTAINING AND EDUCATING

The video game Minecraft was introduced to a school curriculum in Sweden. Teachers believed it taught students about town planning and environmental issues. The game is so popular that over 10 million years of game play has been accumulated across the globe.

THE LONG GAME

Studies have shown that people who play video games spend around 6 – 8 hours per week playing. More than half of all gamers have admitted missing sleep as a result of their gaming habit, while a third have said they have missed a meal.

GAMING FOR A CURE

A group of gamers used a free game called 'Foldit' to help to decode the structure of HIV, which is the virus that causes AIDS. Scientists had been working on the problem for over 10 years – the gamers solved it in 10 days!

A HEDGEHOG GENE

Sonic Hedgehog might sound like the blue hedgehog intent on racing around collecting gold rings, but it is also the name of a gene (a part of your DNA) that plays a role in cell growth and ensures body parts form in the correct position.

Amazing
Molecules and Chemical Reactions

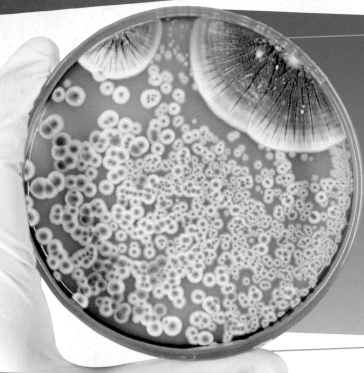

Fantastic Fleming

British scientist Alexander Fleming stumbled upon penicillin when he saw no bacteria were growing around an area of mould in one petri dish. His discovery led to the development of the world's first antibiotic. Some estimates say that over 200 million lives have been saved due to this discovery!

Mpemba Effect

In the correct conditions, hot water appears to freeze more quickly than cold water. While scientists had observed this phenomenon for centuries, it took a schoolboy – Erasto Mpemba from Tanzania – to bring it to the attention of the world. His teacher didn't believe him, but a visiting physicist tested the effect in his laboratory and got the same results.

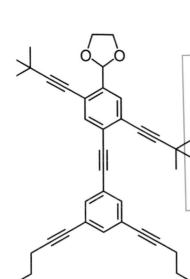

Molecule People

Experts in chemistry have made strings of molecules that look like little people – they often look as though they are dancing, sometimes in pairs. They are called NanoPutians!

Giant Molecules Hit the Road

You may think that molecules – collections of atoms of the same type – are too small to be seen by the naked eye. But the next time you see a car tyre, you will actually be looking at one big molecule!

Why is the Statue of Liberty green?

When copper comes into contact with water, oxygen and carbon dioxide, over time it changes colour – to green. This is why many statues and buildings you see in towns and cities have a greenish tinge.

HOW DOES THE

Cola and Chewy Mint Fountain WORK?

You may have seen a video of this—or you may have done it yourself. You take some chewy mint sweets and drop them into a bottle of cola. A jet of foam will then spray high into the air. It's an impressive experiment, but how does it work?

When a **FIZZY DRINK** is made, carbon dioxide is pumped into the bottles under pressure. When you open the bottle, it releases the pressure and bubbles of carbon dioxide gas form, making the drink fizzy. Adding **CHEWY MINT** sweets to a freshly opened bottle of cola massively speeds up the formation of bubbles and increases the number of **GAS BUBBLES** made.

If you looked at one of the chewy mint sweets under a microscope, you'd find part of the answer: while they might look and feel smooth, these sweets are actually covered in dimples and crevices, giving them a very large surface area. When a sweet is dropped into a fizzy drink, the **CARBON DIOXIDE** in the drink finds that it has a lot of area to attach to, which is what creates the **FOAMING FOUNTAIN OF FROTH.** Different fizzy drinks give different results—diet soda drinks create much taller fountains compared to full-sugar drinks.

Pioneering
MINDS

TYCHO BRAHE
Famous 16th century Danish astronomer Tycho Brahe lost his nose in a swordfight and wore a metal nose for the rest of his life.

ISAAC NEWTON
The scientist who discovered gravity and gave us the laws of motion also poked himself in the eye with a needle. Newton had done this while studying optics and to see the effects it had on the colours he observed. He even drew a picture of his experiment, so we know he actually did it!

LEONARDO DA VINCI

As well as painting the *Mona Lisa,* Leonardo was a scientist and inventor. He was so secretive he wrote his notes in mirror writing (writing in reverse – so the words can only be read when viewed held up to a mirror) to stop people copying him!

Mirror Writing

PARACELCUS

Paracelcus, a 16th century scientist and physician, helped to lay the foundation of modern medicine. He was an alchemist and he devised recipes for creating a tiny living person, called a homunculus.

JOSE DELGADO

This scientist once stopped a charging bull by activating electrodes that he had implanted in the bull's brain. He also convinced 25 people to have 'mind-controlling' electrodes put in their brains.

81

Mindboggling
BUILDINGS

The **COLOSSEUM** in **ROME, ITALY,** is almost **2,000 YEARS OLD!** This amazing **AMPHITHEATRE** could seat approximately **50,000 SPECTATORS.**

Flick to page 93 for more colossal Colosseum facts.

Built from metal and glass, the modern **ENOSHIMA SEA CANDLE** in Japan changes colour depending on the season. On a clear day, you are also able to see Mount Fuji from its observation deck.

LIGHTING
THE PATH TO SAFETY

Jeju City in South Korea wasn't horsing around when it built these two lighthouses, representing Jeju Island's native pony. One red, one white, both have lanterns on their heads and are popular tourist attractions.

TOWER OF HERCULES
is the oldest lighthouse in the world. Built in Spain by the Romans in the 1st century AD, it became a UNESCO World Heritage site in 2009.

CREAC'H lighthouse in France is one of the most powerful lighthouses in the world. Its light beam reaches 59 kilometres away and its foghorn can be heard from 29 kilometres.

Known as 'the lighthouse at the end of the world', **LES ECLAIREURS** is located 9.3 kilometres east of Ushuaia, Argentina, the southernmost city in the world, and can only be reached by boat.

BELL ROCK is known as one of the seven wonders of the industrial world. For over 200 years it has stood on a rock in the North Sea with no reconstruction work on its structure needed.

JEDDAH LIGHT in Saudi Arabia stands 133 metres tall and is the tallest lighthouse in the world. It's not only a lighthouse but the control tower for Jeddah seaport.

SECRETS within

Secret doors and passageways are something characters often discover in books and films. But all of these places are hiding secrets too...

Having a view of the **EIFFEL TOWER** from your living room would be nice, but can you imagine the view from living inside it? Gustave Eiffel, the designer of the tower, did just that! He built an apartment at the top of the tower and no one but him has ever used it.

‹‹‹

The **EMPIRE STATE BUILDING** attracts over 4 million visitors a year who come to view the magnificent Manhattan skyline from its 86th and 102nd floor observation platforms. But just out of reach, unless you are a celebrity or engineer, is the hidden 103rd floor which only has a narrow walkway and no protection from the weather.

›››

In bustling **Trafalgar Square,** London, it would be easy to walk by this unassuming lamppost. But if you look closely, you'll actually see it was hollowed out to house a tiny police station, in the late 1920s to monitor protestors. The tiny prison could only hold two prisoners at a time!

There are many old houses lining the canals of Amsterdam but there is one that holds a significant secret in its attic: a small, fully functioning church called **'OUR LORD IN THE ATTIC'.**
In the 17th century, when Dutch Catholics were persecuted, this hidden church allowed 150 people to secretly worship by entering through a false wall in the living room.

Totally **WEIRD!**

Under the grand Waldorf Astoria hotel in New York is 'Track 61', a secret railroad line used by President Franklin D Roosevelt during World War II.

SKY HIGH WORSHIP

To get to **Taung Kalat** in Myanmar, you need to climb 777 steps whilst passing by the many monkeys that live there. It is believed to be the home of 37 Mahagiri nats or animist spirits!

The gravity-defying **Hanging Temple** near Mount Heng, China is more than 1,500 years old. It is the only temple known to combine the main three traditional Chinese religions: Buddhism, Taoism and Confucianism.

Built on top of a volcanic plug 85 metres high in AD 969, **Saint Michel d'Aiguilhe Chapel** in France is only accessible by climbing 268 stone steps that were carved into the rock face.

Orthodox monasteries at Meteora, Greece, were so difficult to get to that priests were hoisted up the cliff-side in baskets. Its name means 'suspended in the air' in Greek.

Paro Taktsang, also known as the 'Tiger's Nest Temple', is one of the holiest sites in Bhutan. Built into a cliff face 900 metres above the Paro Valley and 3,120 metres above sea level; it takes at least two-hours to hike to.

What's Inside
WINCHESTER HOUSE?

From the outside you might think the Winchester House isn't too out of the ordinary; but behind its impressive exterior hides an architectural labyrinth.

Totally **WEIRD!**

People believe Sarah carried out this continuous work after a medium told her that she would be followed and haunted by ghosts. The maze-like design would confuse them and give her some peace!

When William Wirt Winchester died in 1881, he left his wife Sarah US $20 million—a fortune that is equivalent to around US $500 million today. In 1884, Sarah bought an unfinished, eight-bedroom farmhouse in San Jose, California.

With her fortune, she got to work on her construction project. For 38 years, until her death in 1922, Sarah hired carpenters to work day and night, seven days a week, on her bizarre plans. What was created was an unfinished seven-story mansion that had rooms added on in strange places, staircases that led to nowhere, trapdoors and secret passageways. There was even an odd and dangerous door on the first floor that opened out onto nothing but a deadly drop to the grounds below!

Sarah also had an obsession with the number 13. No one knows why, but many aspects of her house revolved around the number 13 including 13-step stairways, 13-paned windows and 13-paneled ceilings. Even the mansion's 13th bathroom had 13 windows in it!

13

The house included:
- 2,230 square metres
- 10,000 windows
- 2,000 doors
- 160 rooms
- 52 skylights
- 47 stairways and fireplaces
- 17 chimneys
- 13 bathrooms
- 6 kitchens
- Cost US $5 million dollars in 1923 or US $71 million today

FORBIDDEN CITY

Where: Beijing, China
Built: 1420
Visitors: 17,000,000+

DID YOU KNOW? Clever design means birds cannot land on the roofs of the Forbidden City!

LINCOLN MEMORIAL

Where: Washington DC, USA
Built: 1914–1922
Visitors: 7,900,000

DID YOU KNOW? There used to be a spelling mistake on the North Wall! Whoops!

COLOGNE CATHEDRAL

Where: Cologne, Germany
Built: 1248–1560
Visitors: 6,000,000

DID YOU KNOW? During World War II it was hit by 14 bombs and still did not collapse!

PETERHOF PALACE

Where: St Petersburg, Russia
Built: 1714–1723
Visitors: 5,245,900

DID YOU KNOW? Peterhof's Grand Cascade water feature includes 64 different waterfalls and 200 statues.

PARTHENON

Where: Athens, Greece
Built: 447–438 BC
Visitors: 7,200,000

DID YOU KNOW? The Parthenon is earthquake resistant.

PALACE OF VERSAILLES

Where: Versailles, France
Built: 1631–1634
Visitors: 8,100,000

DID YOU KNOW? There are 357 mirrors in the Hall of Mirrors inside the palace!

EIFFEL TOWER

Where: Paris, France
Built: 1887–1889
Visitors: 7,000,000

DID YOU KNOW? In cold weather the Eiffel Tower shrinks around 15 centimetres.

TAJ MAHAL

Where: Agra, India
Built: 1632–1653
Visitors: 7,090,207

DID YOU KNOW? Taj Mahal means 'Crown Palace' in Urdu.

COLOSSEUM

Where: Rome, Italy
Built: AD 70–80
Visitors: 7,600,000

DID YOU KNOW? The colosseum is the largest amphitheatre in the world!

ST. PETER'S BASILICA

Where: Vatican City, Rome
Built: 1506–1626
Visitors: 11,000,000

DID YOU KNOW? The 'paintings' inside the Basilica are actually mosaics!

93

Where's a better place to find a pair of shoes than in a **giant shoe box?** This shop was created as a pop-up store for a music festival in Barcelona, Spain.

They SELL what?

THESE BUILDLINGS HAVE BEEN DESIGNED TO GIVE A CLUE ABOUT WHAT GOES ON INSIDE OF THEM.

Found on a **PINEAPPLE** farm in Bathurst, South Africa, this is the world's biggest pineapple building standing at 17 metres.

The **Toad Museum** in Yasothon, Thailand showcases the legend of a local Prince (the toad prince) who saved humans from being flooded by defeating the god of rain.

Totally WEIRD!

When buildings are designed to look like the objects that they are selling it is called novelty architecture!

This **ICE CREAM** company can be found in Florida, USA. Their cone-shaped buildings measure over 7.5 metres tall!

There's something **FISHY** about the **National Fisheries Development** building in Hyderabad, India, built in 2012.

The 12-metre tall **Gibeau Orange Julep** restaurant has been standing in Montreal, Canada since 1966! Its nickname is '**The Big Orange**.'

Start your engines!
Karl Schwanzer designed **BMW's** headquarters in Munich, Germany to look like the company's **four-cylinder engine.**

BRILLIANT BRIDGES

The Rolling Bridge over part of London's Grand Union Canal doesn't really roll...but it does curl up into an octagon thanks to a special system built into its handrails. You can see the bridge roll itself up every Wednesday and Friday at noon, and on Saturdays at 2 pm!

The **Eshima Ohashi Bridge** in Japan might look as if you're driving into the sky; but it's only an optical illusion! From certain angles it looks like the bridge is rising at 45°, but it actually only has around a 6% incline.

Don't tie yourself up in knots! The **Lucky Knot Bridge** in China is multi levelled and 'knots' roads, parks and riverbanks together. It was designed to look like the traditional Chinese art of knot-tying which symbolises luck and prosperity.

A street artist created the **Lego Bridge** in Wuppertal, Germany by giving a normal concrete structure a creative makeover. The artist and his team used colourful paint to make the bridge resemble Lego blocks.

Pont Gustave-Flaubert Bridge in France is unlike other bridges as instead of it opening like a drawbridge to let boats pass, the road lifts straight up thanks to a pulley system. It takes around 12 minutes to lift the bridge all the way up!

Would you like to see a dragon breathe fire? On weekends in Vietnam this **Dragon Bridge** does exactly that! Dragons are important in Asian culture, symbolising power, nobility and prosperity.

Built in
REFRIGERATION

Halfway between mainland Norway and the North Pole, on one of the northernmost inhabited islands in the world, you'll find SVALBARD GLOBAL SEED VAULT.

Built over an astounding 120 metres into **the side of an icy mountain,** this long-term storage facility is often referred to as the **'Doomsday vault'** as it was built to outlive any man-made or natural disaster, and holds one of the most vital natural resources to mankind—**crops.**

From **rice** to **lettuce,** the Seed Vault has the capacity to hold **4.5 million** varieties of crop, and currently holds over **1 million samples** from nearly every country in the world! Samples need to be kept at **-18°C** to ensure their survival, so **Svalbard** was the perfect location to build this underground storage facility as the outside temperature and permafrost helps to **naturally freeze** the building, making it cost effective.

Get a
MOVE ON!

CHAPTER 6

Once, an **ENVELOPE** containing **£15,000 CASH** was left on the **LONDON TUBE.**

Zoom to page 108 to discover more items left behind on London's Tube.

← Measuring at **2.05 metres** long, **Ebenezer Place** in **Wick**, Scotland, has held the record for the world's shortest street since 2006. The street only has one address!

↑ **Spreuerhofstrasse** in **Reutlingen**, Germany, is the world's narrowest street, measuring **50 centimetres** at its widest and **31 centimetres** at its narrowest point! That's one tight squeeze!

RADICAL ROADS
AND STREETS

Baldwin Street in **Dunedin**, New Zealand, has a gradient of **34.8%** and is the steepest street in the world. Every year people race up and down the street in the Baldwin Street Gutbuster foot race. →

Since 1960, Brazil has been able to boast of having the world's widest street. The **Monumental Axis** in Brazil's capital, Brasilia, is **250 metres** wide and has six traffic lanes.

Nicknamed **'Death Road'**, until 2006 the North Yungas Road was the only road between the Yungas region of **Bolivia** and the capital city, Le Paz. Only **3.5 metres wide** and without guard rails, it was considered the **most dangerous road in the world.** It is now mostly used as a cycle route – **a very scary one.**

Cutting through a whopping **14 countries** and spanning around **30,431 kilometres**, the **Pan-American Highway** is the world's longest road, starting in **Alaska** and ending in **Argentina!** That's one long road trip!

103

Horse-drawn taxi cabs called **FIAKER** have been all the rage in Vienna since the 17th century.

CATCH A CAB!

Hop in to **TAXIS** from around the world!

Captains of **H2O TAXI** in Victoria, Canada, sometimes twirl their boats in time with each other to perform water ballets!

The **BICITAXI** (electric bike taxi) found in Mexico City is an eco-friendly way to travel around the busy city.

COCOTAXI in Cuba are three wheeled, yellow and shaped like a coconut!

Totally **WEIRD!**

Going on a 5-kilometre taxi ride will cost you, on average, £0.75 in Egypt but a whopping £20 in Switzerland!

There are nearly 14,000 iconic **YELLOW TAXIS** on the roads in New York City.

CICLOTAXIS CDMX

MÉXICO

Brightly coloured **TUK TUKS** are a quick and fun way to get around busy cities in Thailand.

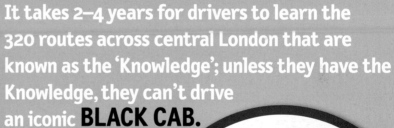

It takes 2–4 years for drivers to learn the 320 routes across central London that are known as the 'Knowledge'; unless they have the Knowledge, they can't drive an iconic **BLACK CAB.**

With more canals than roads, **WATER TAXIS** are the fastest way to move around Venice, Italy compared to traditional taxis.

COULD YOU OUTRUN A HORSE?

In 1980, in a pub in the Welsh town of **LLANWRTYD WELLS**, landlord **Gordon Green** overheard two customers arguing over whether humans could outrun a horse in a long-distance race. From this argument the **Man versus Horse** marathon was born!

Every June, starting from the original pub, the **NEUADD ARMS**, participants from all around the world must compete over a **22-mile** stretch of tough terrain with steep hills and bogs. Competitors on foot run alongside around **60 horses** (with riders) each year to see who will be victorious.

You may think, 'no way could a person beat a horse,' but over the race's 40-year history, two people have done just that! **Huw Lobb** in 2004 was the first, beating horse **Kay Bee Jay** by 2 minutes and 17 seconds. For this he won **£25,000**, a prize pot that had been growing by £1,000 each year until a runner won. In 2007, **Florian Holzinger** was the next winner, beating the fastest horse, **Lucy**, by an incredible 11 minutes!

DID YOU KNOW?
Lobb credited his win to being faster at running down hills than the horses.

Totally WEIRD!

The fastest ever recorded running speed of a horse is 88 km/h.

Left Behind in
LONDON

Every year the **Transport for London lost property office** sorts through over **300,000 items** that have been **left behind** on the capital's **Tube, trains** and **buses.**

Most of these items are everyday objects and include over:

14,000 KEYS

36,000 TELEPHONES

7,500 UMBRELLAS

49,000 BAGS

But there is also a trove of bizarre items that include:

AN **URN** OF **ASHES**

A JUDGE'S **WIG**

A HAIRDRESSING **MANNEQUIN HEAD**

DID YOU KNOW?

Roughly 22% of the objects handed in are returned to their rightful owners.

A **PROSTHETIC** LEG

A **DRUM** KIT

A LIFE-SIZE **SPIDERMAN DOLL**

Putting the Fun in FUNICULAR

Climbing to the top of a very steep hill or mountain can be tough and tiring, so in the mid-19th century funicular railways were specially designed to make light work of the slopes. This clever system involves two passenger cars on tracks, attached at opposite ends by the same cable. The cable is wound around a pulley system, so that when one car is being pulled up the slope, the other car is being lowered at the same time.

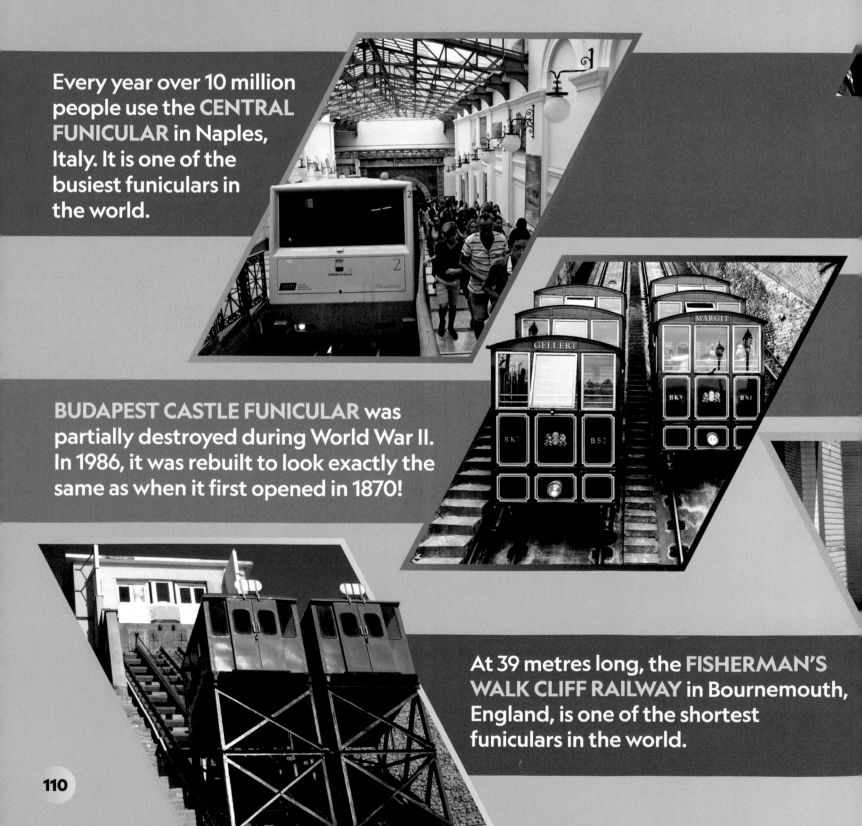

Every year over 10 million people use the **CENTRAL FUNICULAR** in Naples, Italy. It is one of the busiest funiculars in the world.

BUDAPEST CASTLE FUNICULAR was partially destroyed during World War II. In 1986, it was rebuilt to look exactly the same as when it first opened in 1870!

At 39 metres long, the **FISHERMAN'S WALK CLIFF RAILWAY** in Bournemouth, England, is one of the shortest funiculars in the world.

STOOSBAHN FUNICULAR in Switzerland is the steepest in the world, with a gradient as steep as 110% (47.7°)!

Hanging from rails, **DRESDEN SUSPENSION RAILWAY** in Germany is the only suspended funicular in the world.

The **JOHNSTOWN INCLINED PLANE,** in Pennsylvania, USA, was built as an escape route to higher ground after the catastrophic floods of 1889!

THERE'S SNOW STOPPING ME!

Archaeologists can't quite pinpoint when humans started to use **dog sleds** to travel across snow and ice, but do agree that it has been for thousands of years in the Arctic Circle. **ALASKAN HUSKIES, SIBERIAN HUSKIES** and **ALASKAN MALAMUTES** are used most often to pull sleds.

Prototypes of **SNOWMOBILES** in the early 20th century saw a sled powered by an **aeroplane propeller** and steered by **skis.** Nowadays, they are still steered by skis in the front, but have tracks to drive them forward and a **motorised engine** for power.

KHARKOVCHANKA is an Antarctic off-road campervan that was made by the **Soviet Union** in 1958 to travel to the South Pole and back. It has an **8-bed cabin** inside, as well as a kitchen and toilet!

In 3.5 seconds, the luxury **RIPSAW EV TANK** can reach speeds of 97 km/h meaning it can accelerate **faster** than most cars! Originally designed for the **military,** people can now buy a civilian version, minus the armour!

CROSS-COUNTRY SKIING originates in **Scandinavia.** It is not only a sport, but a means of travel and recreation. Cross-country skiers can be faster than other modes of transport on the harsh terrain.

DID YOU KNOW?

Ludvig Søgnen Jensen holds the world record for 100-metre ski sprint at 11.03 seconds!

SECRETLY SEARCHING

DID YOU KNOW?

Scientists predict that the whole wreck of *Titanic* could disappear by 2030, due to bacteria eating away at it!

In 1912, the world's largest passenger ship of its time, *Titanic*, collided with an iceberg on her maiden voyage and sank to the bottom of the Atlantic Ocean. For many years after this tragic accident, sonar expeditions mapping the sea floor were unsuccessful in locating the wreckage.

It wasn't until 1985 that Robert Ballard found *Titanic* by using a new technique. He realised using only sonar would not help him find the wreckage, so he used cameras on a deep-sea vehicle to look for large pieces of debris and followed these like a breadcrumb trail until he found the wreckage, which was 612 kilometres southeast of Newfoundland, Canada.

The discovery made headlines around the world and everyone was fascinated with the find. But it wasn't until recently that we found out Ballard wasn't actually on a mission to find the *Titanic*, this was just a cover story! He was actually on a top-secret Cold War mission for the United Stated Navy and President Ronald Reagan.

His mission was to study and recover two wrecked Cold War nuclear submarines, the *U.S.S Thresher* and *U.S.S Scorpion*. Ballard completed his mission 12 days early, so used the remaining time to search for *Titanic*, which was conveniently located between the two submarine wrecks!

Since *Titanic's* discovery many expeditions have taken place. Thousands of items have been salvaged such as jewellery, clothes and furniture.

TANTALISING
TUNNELS

The **Bund Sightseeing Tunnel,** under the Huangpu River in Shanghai, China, is **short** but **strange**. Automated cars ferry passengers through a tunnel filled with **psychedelic lights** and weird audio-visual effects. The ride is meant to represent a **journey to the centre** of the **Earth.**

Totally **WEIRD!**

In Guizhou Province, China, there is a strange road tunnel that sends people back in time! Many drivers report that after driving through the tunnel the clock on their mobile phones has gone back by exactly 60 minutes!

CHANNEL TUNNEL

Connecting **England** and **France,** the 50 kilometres Channel Tunnel is the **world's longest international** tunnel. Although built by both the **English** and **French,** more of the tunnel was dug from the English side.

TUNNEL LOG

The unusual **Tunnel Log** in Sequoia National Park, California, was created in 1938 after a giant **2,000-year-old Sequoia tree** fell and blocked the road. Instead of moving the tree, they **carved out** a tunnel for cars to drive through!

GUOLIANG TUNNEL

Guoliang Tunnel in **China** was built by hand into the side of the Taihang Mountains by **13 Guoliang villagers.** The tunnel is jagged and steep due to the tools used, and is known as 'the road that does not tolerate any mistakes'.

LÆRDAL TUNNEL

Lærdal, Norway, is home to the **world's longest road tunnel** at 24.5 kilometres. The tunnel takes **20 minutes** to drive through! To make it less boring for drivers, the tunnel is split into **sections** with **coloured lighting** and **caverns.**

Out of this WORLD

CHAPTER 7

URANUS was the **FIRST PLANET** to be **DISCOVERED** using a **TELESCOPE.**

Blast over to page 125 to uncover more facts on Uranus.

High Fliers

The first creatures to go to space were not humans or dogs or chimps. They were flies. Seventy-five years ago, scientists put fruit flies in an old rocket from World War II and fired it into space. They didn't send humans as they were afraid that cosmic radiation might mutate or kill the astronauts. When the rocket came back down to Earth, the scientists saw that the flies had survived. And none of them were mutants.

Animal Astronauts

Space Zoo

Lots of different animals have been sent into space. Bees, flies, wasps, fish, turtles, monkeys, chimpanzees, dogs, cats, mice, rats, rabbits, frogs, newts, guinea pigs, spiders, geckos and even jellyfish have all been rocketed off the face of Earth! Tardigrades (left – also known as water bears) were able to survive for 10 days in space (with no tardigrade spacesuit except their own bodies).

Wasps

TORTOISES
on the Moon?

In 1968, a year before Neil Armstrong and Buzz Aldrin became the first people to set foot on the Moon, a Russian space probe sent two tortoises. The tortoises orbited the Moon and returned to Earth unharmed. During the mission, Russian cosmonauts decided to play a little prank on the Americans by pretending that there were people on board and that Russia was about to win the race to the Moon!

Rabbits

Frogs

Floating in a Tin Can

People in orbit are not free of the pull of Earth's gravity – they're actually falling, but forever. Because of this, astronauts on the International Space Station (the ISS) don't feel gravity's effect on them.

Only around 550 people have ever been to space – that's 0.000007% of the world's population. And, so far, only 12 people have ever walked on the moon.

While in Space, astronauts are subjected to much weaker gravitational forces (microgravity). Humans did not evolve to live with this reduced force of gravity and the longer they stay in space, the more severe and long lasting the effects can be on an astronaut's health. The eyesight of some astronauts on the ISS gets worse as a result of being in space for a long time. Microgravity also causes astronauts to get taller – up to 5 centimetres!

When astronauts return to Earth they feel pretty sea sick. Being cemented back to the ground makes many astronauts dizzy to the extent that they can't stand up on their own for more than 10 minutes without fainting.

Our muscles need gravity. In space, astronauts need to do 2 hours of exercise 6 days a week to try to keep their muscles from wasting away.

If you're an astronaut, every month you spend in space could mean losing 1% of your bone mass.

THE CENTRE OF OUR SOLAR SYSTEM

The centre of our Solar System is not the Sun! The Sun actually orbits the centre of our Solar System.

The SUNNY SYSTEM

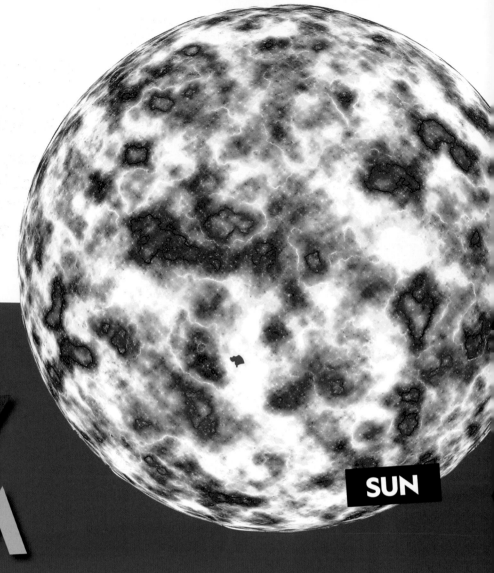

SUN

HOT and COLD

MERCURY

Mercury, the closest planet to the Sun, gets very hot in the daytime – about twice as hot as your oven – (430°C) but has chilly night times (–180°C).

NEIGHBOURS

Mercury, despite being the closest planet to the Sun, spends most of its time closer to Earth than Venus!

EARTH

SLOW PLUTO

Pluto is less than a year old! Well, kind of. Since its discovery in the 20th century, Pluto (a dwarf planet) has yet to complete one orbit around the Sun.

PLUTO

ROTTEN EGGS

Uranus, the 7th planet from the Sun, smells like rotten eggs!

THE WINDS OF NEPTUNE

The fastest winds ever observed were winds of methane gas on Neptune – travelling at 2,000 kilometres per hour, or over 500 metres per second!

NEPTUNE

LONG DAY

Venus has a long day. It takes 243 Earth days for Venus to rotate once on its axis. A day on Venus is longer than its year!

VENUS

SHARKS
vs
SATURN

New evidence suggests Saturn's rings may be less than 100 million years old, which means sharks have been around for much longer.

Fly Me To The
MOON
(and BACK)

Ashes to Ashes

Eugene Shoemaker is the only human scattered on the Moon. His ashes were scattered near the Moon's south pole. Shoemaker was a geologist who trained astronauts on the Apollo missions. He also confirmed that the craters on the Moon and on Earth were caused by asteroid impacts.

Hot Days and Chilly Nights

In the sunshine, the surface of the Moon can be hot: over 100°C! At night-time, the temperature drops to –153°C.

Further and Further Away

The Moon is moving further and further away from the Earth. Every year it is pushed nearly 4 centimetres further away from us.

Moon Garbage

Humans have left over 180,000 kilograms of stuff on the Moon, including crashed satellites, old moon buggies, tools, an astronauts' family photograph and even human waste!

MODERN MOON ART

There is a tiny art gallery on the Moon. It is on a small ceramic wafer. It had to be smuggled on board Apollo 12 and features artworks (one of them, a rude drawing you might only expect to see in a public toilet).

Cosmic Connectivity

Next time you're searching for a network connection, remember that the Moon has **wi-fi.** Through a combination of telescopes, satellites and lasers, the Moon has pretty good upload and download speeds!

Wi Fi

Sharp Dust

Moon dust is so sharp and fine that it can penetrate the top layers of an astronaut's space suit.

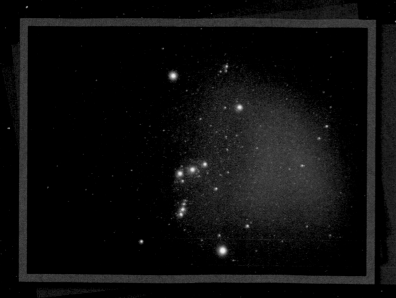

ORION'S SWORD

The constellation Orion – one of the most easily recognised in the night sky of the northern hemisphere – hides a secret. One of its 'stars' is not a star, but a nebula (a cloud of gas and dust). Orion's Nebula is in the 'sword' that hangs below Orion's belt. The nebula is huge – some estimates are as large as 30 light years across and is quite close to us (it's only around 1300 light years away from Earth).

COOL COSMOS!

Neutron Stars

Neutron Stars helped humans to test Einstein's theory of Relativity and they are about the closest anything can get to being a black hole, without actually being one. First off, they are small (the whole star can be only 20 kilometres across) and they are very, very heavy. A tablespoon of our Sun would weigh about as much as 5 bags of sugar. A tablespoon of a Neutron Star would weigh as much as Mount Everest.

CURVY STARS

Scientists have recently discovered that our galaxy – the Milky Way – is not just a flat disk that bulges in the middle but is shaped more like a Pringle!

WHERE DOES GOLD COME FROM?

Scientists believe that 80% of the gold (and other heavy metals) on Earth was formed by massive dying stars called 'collapsars'. The other 20% comes from colliding neutron stars. The gold available to humans was delivered by asteroids soon after Earth formed.

THE SMELL OF SPACE

NASA chemists developed a perfume based on the smells that astronauts have reported after going on spacewalks. And apparently, space smells like burned steak, gunpowder and raspberries! NASA used the scent for astronaut training – now it's available to buy.

BLACK HOLE SUN

The brightest object ever discovered in the Universe is from a black hole – a quasar black hole. The light from the quasar black hole is also old, having travelled across the universe for 13 billion years before reaching us.

The Death of the Sun

Our Sun is about **halfway** through its life. It is so hot in the Sun that hydrogen atoms are fused together. In about **5 billion years**, the Sun will start to run out of this hydrogen fuel. When it does, it will *grow* in size – and will consume all of the inner planets of the Solar System (including Earth) in the process.

STAR MAKERS

The Largest Thing In the Universe

There is a wall in space that is the largest thing we have ever discovered. The Hercules–Corona Borealis Great Wall is a collection of dust, gas and thousands of galaxies. It measures a whopping 10 billion light years in length!

That's a lot of birthdays

The oldest star known to humans is the Methuselah star. It is believed to be over **14 billion years old!**

Most of the Universe is Missing

All of the millions of stars and galaxies that we can see in the sky make up only a tiny percentage **(about 4% we think)** of the total universe. The rest is 'dark matter' and **'dark energy'**. We call these things **'dark'** because, at the moment, we have no idea what they are made of!

Planets, Planets, Everywhere

It has only been 30 years since humans proved that planets exist beyond our Solar System. In 1992 the existence of the first two 'exoplanets' – a planet that has a different sun to ours – were confirmed. Now, astronomers have found over 4,000 exoplanets and think that most stars are likely to have planets orbiting them, which puts the number of possible planets in our own galaxy – the Milky Way – in the billions!

How I wonder what you are?

Stars don't twinkle! They look like they twinkle because of changes in the Earth's atmosphere that distort the star's light before it reaches our eyes.

Sporting
SUPERSTARS

For over **30 YEARS,** JAPAN has hosted an **ANNUAL SNOWBALL FIGHTING COMPETITION.**

Read more about snowball fights on page 138.

1904
OLYMPIC
MARATHON

Totally **WEIRD!**

Marathon running was inspired by a story from Ancient Greece when a messenger ran 40 kilometres from the site of 'Marathon' to Athens to announce the Greeks had claimed victory over a Persian army. Modern marathons last slightly longer than this distance – 42.195 kilometres. The extra distance is attributed to the 1908 Olympic Games in London, where Queen Alexandra of the United Kingdom wanted the original distance increased so the race could start at Windsor Castle and end at the royal box in the Olympic Stadium.

The Olympic Games in 1904 were the first to award gold, silver and bronze medals for first, second and third places. 1904 was also the first time that the Olympics were held in a country outside of Europe. They were awarded to the city of Chicago, USA but ended up being held in St Louis. One of the amazing facts about the Olympics was the fact that six medals were won by a gymnast with a wooden leg!

The Olympic marathon was truly bizarre. American Fred Lorz was the first person across the finish line but he didn't win the race. This was because he hitched a ride for part of the course! The real winner – a man named Thomas Hicks – took just under three-and-a-half hours to complete the race and nearly died in the process. Despite suffering from heat exhaustion (temperatures were over 30°C), Hicks was not allowed to drink water.

One of the marathon runners turned up in normal work-clothes and ordinary shoes. Representing Cuba, Felix Carvajal also suffered from the heat, humidity and lack of drinking water so decided to eat some apples from a nearby orchard. The apples were rotten and gave him terrible stomach pains, so he lay down and had a nap. When he woke up, he carried on running. He came fourth! Another runner in the marathon was chased a mile off course by wild dogs! Of the 32 athletes who started the marathon, only 14 actually managed to finish it.

GOING
THE DISTANCE

TOUR DE FRANCE

In **1903,** the first **Tour de France** long-distance cycling race was held. At that time, the bicycle was a relatively new invention (the first bicycle being the **'Draisine'** invented by a **German Baron** in **1817** – however, it had no pedals). The first race was **2,428 kilometres** in length; now, it stretches over **3,200 kilometres** and the course extends to other countries. Cyclists in the race can lose between 1 and 2 litres of sweat per hour – **120 litres** in total: enough over the course of the race to flush a toilet over **16** times!

YAK ATTACK

The **Yak Attack** (named after the relatives of long-haired cattle that live in **Nepal**) is the world's highest cycle race. Although the **280-kilometre** race is far shorter than other endurance cycle races, the Yak Attack involves racers climbing over a total of **9,000 metres** – higher than Mount Everest!

KEEP ON RUNNING

In **2016**, British comedian **Eddie Izzard** ran **27** marathons in **27** days around **South Africa**, raising over a million pounds for charity in the process. That's over **1,100** kilometres in less than a month! Rory Coleman ran **28** marathons in **28** days in **2013** and ran **43** ultramarathons (double the length of a normal marathon) in **43** days in **2004.**

ICE MARATHONS

For those who want more of a challenge in their marathons, consider the **Antarctic marathon** – the world's most southerly race, which takes place on the **coldest continent** on Earth. There is also a **North Pole marathon**, which takes place on the frozen **Arctic Ocean!**

WINTER SPORTS

SKELETON OR LUGE?

If racing on a board face-first a few centimetres above an icy track is your thing, then the skeleton is for you. Riding a similar sled face up and feet-first is the winter sport of luge, and it is actually more dangerous than skeleton. In either case, riders can reach speeds of over **120 kph!**

SNOWBALL!

'**Yukigassen**' is a Japanese word that means 'Snowball fight'. Yukigassen is a snowball fighting competition where two teams of seven players compete, with players eliminated from the game when hit with a snowball. Snowballing took off as an organised sport in **1989**, with the first tournament pitting **70** teams of fighters against each other.

SPEEDY SKIS

One of the fastest winter sports is downhill alpine skiing, in which skiers can reach speeds of over **160 kph!**

KAYAK THE SLOPES

Snow kayaking takes the water-sport of kayaking to snowy mountaintops. Kayakers use their rowing paddles, but don't need to bother with a life-vest.

SKIJORING

Skiers being dragged by dogs or horses are '**skijoring**'. Races usually range between 5 and 20 kilometres. Think of the poor dogs that have to do all of the running and pulling!

GRAB A SHOVEL

Some people like to launch themselves down a snowy slope with nothing more than a snow shovel to act as a sled. If you don't have a shovel, why not try a wok instead? Wok sled racing sits racers in woks speeding up to **100 kph**.

139

Reach for the SKY!

AT THE AGE OF 8, PRODIGY SKY BROWN BECAME THE YOUNGEST COMPETITOR TO EVER TAKE PART IN THE US OPEN SKATEBOARDING COMPETITION. AT THE AGE OF 10, SKY BECAME THE YOUNGEST EVER PROFESSIONAL SKATEBOARDER IN THE WORLD!

In her short but successful career, Sky has competed around the globe, on continents such as North America, Europe, Asia and South America. At the World Skateboarding Championships in Sao Paulo, Brazil, Sky finished third and scooped a bronze medal.

Sky started skating while at preschool and has worked hard for her success. From an early age, she learned her skateboarding skills without a professional trainer. Instead, Sky watched hours and hours of content online, learning tricks from other skaters on YouTube. Sky is a true self-taught superstar.

Sky even has a skate ramp in her garden to help hone her skills!

141

Martial Arts

You might know of Karate, Judo, Tae Kwon Do, Muay Thai boxing, but have you heard of these martial arts?

Sumo is the national sport of **Japan.** The sport pits two large fighters against each other who use a range of moves and holds to try and push their opponent to the floor or out of the ring. Before the match, **sumo wrestlers** (called **Rishiki**) throw salt into the ring to purify it as **Sumo** is a ritual of the **Shinto** religion as well as being a sport.

SUMO

TAI CHI

Tai Chi is a martial art that was developed in the late 1500s. It is mostly practised as rather slow, elegant, dance-like moves and steps. In **2017, 50,000** people gathered across 200 venues in **Henan, China,** to practise **Tai Chi** in a mass martial art event.

Dating back over **3,000** years, **Kalaripayatti** is one of the world's oldest **martial arts**. Students of this Indian fighting style were taught defence and fighting techniques using their bare hands, and wooden or metallic weapons. It is said that masters of **Kalaripayattu** are able to disable an opponent by striking one of the vital pressure points on the body.

KALARIPAYATTU

DAMBE

Dambe is a **martial art** that comes from **Nigeria**. Its origins date back to the 10th century. Competitors duel over three rounds, using a tightly bound hand known as a 'spear' for attack and the other as a 'shield' for defence.

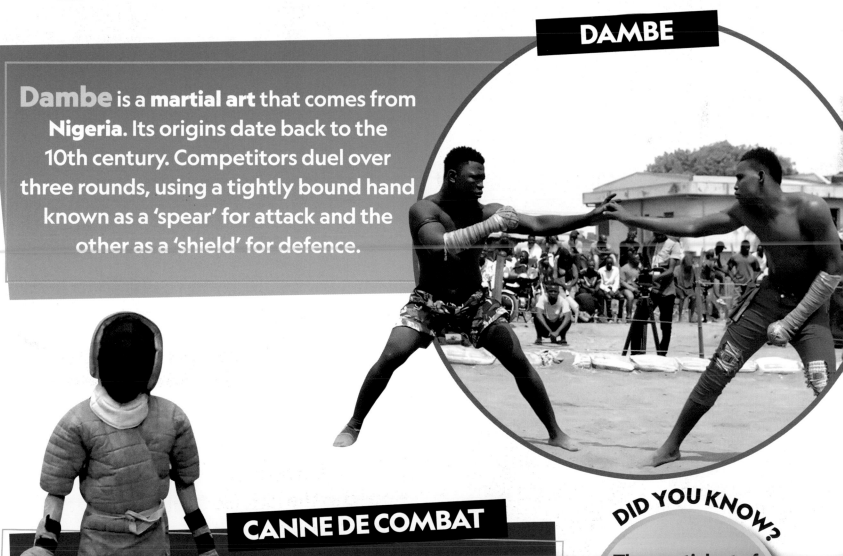

CANNE DE COMBAT

Canne de Combat is a **martial art** from **France**. It teaches methods of self-defence, using walking sticks to strike opponents.

DID YOU KNOW?

The martial art of **Bataireacht** is an ancient method of fighting with sticks that comes from **Ireland**.

BALL CRAZY

Bossaball

The Spanish sport of Bossaball blends football, volleyball and gymnastics. Players try to score points over a net whilst bouncing on a trampoline. The name 'Bossaball' refers to the Bossa Nova music that is played during the game.

Totally **WEIRD!**

The greatest ever defeat in football history happened in 2002 in Madagascar. Playing in the national championships, AS Adema beat Stade Olympique l'Emyrne 149 goals to 0. However, all of the goals for AS Adema were actually made by the opposing team, who made 149 own-goals in a protest about refereeing decisions made in previous games.

Can We Have Our Balls Back?

There are two golf balls on the surface of the moon. American Astronaut Alan Shepard hit both of the balls during a mission to the lunar surface in 1971. He used a makeshift club made with a device for collecting soil samples and a club head and balls smuggled on board the Apollo 14 landing craft inside his spacesuit!

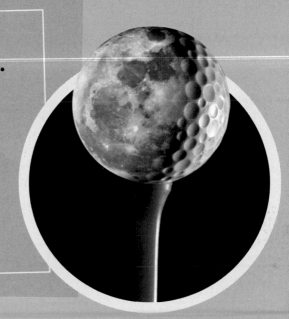

Slamball

The best way to describe slamball is basketball with the addition of trampolines! Competitors soar through the air with added spring, which makes for some sky-high slams.

Wimbledon

Tennis balls at Wimbledon are stored at exactly 20°C to ensure optimum performance. They are then changed every nine games. Used balls are then sold, with money from the sales donated to charity.

Coolly
CREATIVE

There are so many **TWINS** in the NIGERIAN CITY of **IGBO-ORA,** that there is a FESTIVAL celebrating **TWINS** EVERY YEAR.

Flip to page 158 to learn more about fun festivals from around the world.

CHAPTER 9

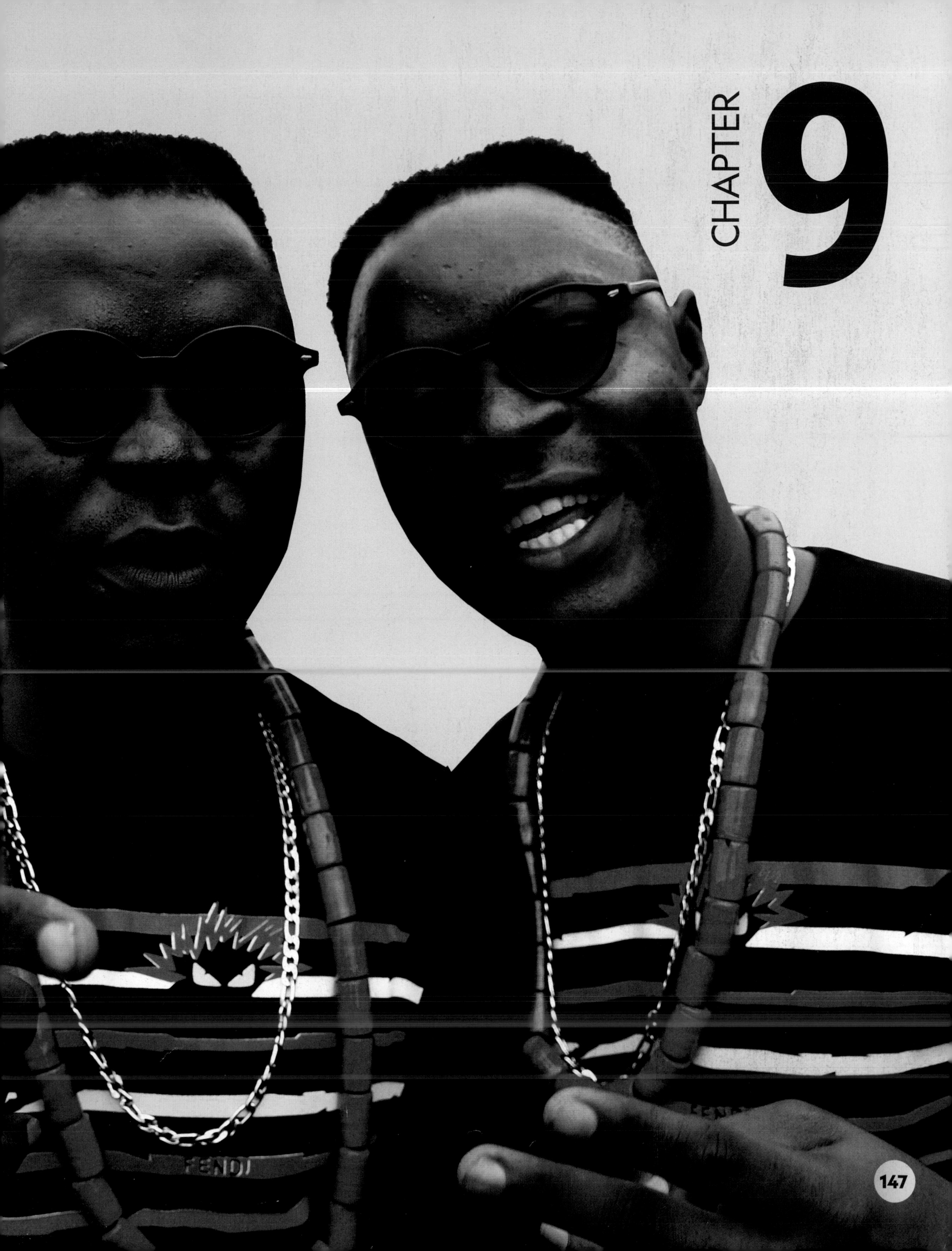

Strangest Sculptures

THE FARTING BULL

Although the sculpture is officially called 'What You See Might Not Be Real' the name of 'Farting Bull' has stuck, for obvious reasons. The artwork, by Chinese artist Chen Wenling, shows a bull, propelled by an explosive fart-cloud, pinning a devil halfway up a wall.

JAWS?

In a small village in southern England, a great white shark can be seen diving through the roof of a house. The Headington Shark (officially called 'Untitled, 1986') was commissioned by journalist Bill Heine's to represent threats from above, such as atomic bombs or nuclear fallout.

KRYPTOS

Calling all spies! 'Kryptos' is a sculpture at the headquarters of the US Central Intelligence Agency that contains four hidden messages. Three of the messages have been decoded, but nobody has yet cracked the meaning hidden of the fourth message.

FLOATING TAPS

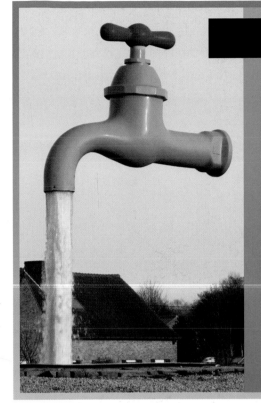

A mixture of sculpture and optical illusion: gigantic taps floating in the air, with water somehow running out of them, can be found in locations all over the world – in Belgium, Spain, Switzerland, Mexico, New Zealand, the USA, Canada and the United Kingdom.

BUDDHA BUILDING

In 2014, two giant, naked Buddha sculptures appeared climbing up the walls of a restaurant in Jinan, a city in China. After locals complained, the statues were taken down, only to reappear two years later!

CHARLES LA TROBE

Many universities have statues of famous people, but a statue in Melbourne, Australia, turns that idea on its head – literally. The statue of Charles La Trobe – the first Lieutenant-Governor of Victoria, is completely upside down!

FIFTY SHADES OF EGG

Dr Seuss's book, *Green Eggs and Ham* was written as a bet. A publisher challenged the author and illustrator to write a book that only used 50 different words. And Dr Seuss did it—writing one of his most famous books ever.

WEIRD WORDS

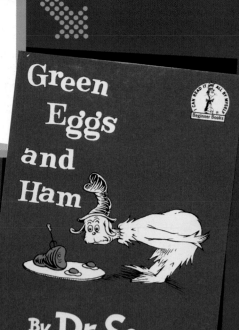

Green Eggs and Ham By Dr. Seuss

ALPHABETICAL ORDER

Alphabetical Africa is a weird book in that chapter 1 only has words that start with the letter 'a'. Chapter 2 has words that start with 'a' and 'b'; chapter 3 adds words starting with 'c'. This continues all the way through to chapter 26. Chapter 27 then removes the 'z's and by chapter 52, all the words start with only 'a' again.

A BOOK NEEDS MORE THAN ONE SENTENCE

Books are made up of chapters, which are made up of paragraphs, which are made up of sentences, which are made up of words. Usually. 'Dancing Lessons for the Advanced in Age' is a novel, written in the 1960s, that only has one sentence. But it is a very long sentence—over 100 pages long!

OLD AND MODERN GIBBERISH

Some books don't make any sense by accident and some do it on purpose. The *Voynich Manuscript* is a text from the 1400s that is written in a language that scholars and professors have been unable to translate. In modern times, the *Codex Seraphinianus*, written by Italian artist Luigi Sefini in 1981, is an encyclopaedia of things that don't exist. It is written in a language made up by the author and so makes no sense at all.

MOST COMMON LETTER? NO THANKS!

'E' is the most commonly used letter in the English language. Try and write a full sentence without it. It isn't easy! But author Ernest Vincent Wright wrote a 50,000-word novel, *Gadsby* without using the letter once! To make sure he didn't accidentally include the letter, the author tied the 'e' key down on his typewriter!

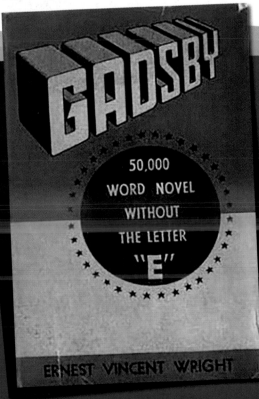

TO BE? NO! NOT TO BE

E-prime is a way of using the English language, but without using any versions of the verb 'to be'. That means not using 'am', 'are', 'be', 'been', 'being', 'is', 'was', and 'were'. Instead of saying 'the door is yellow', e-prime would have you say, 'the door appears yellow to me'. Try it! The idea was to try and make writing clearer, but it never really caught on.

SEA ORGAN

No need for musicians – **waves rolling** into the shore of the Croatian city of **Zadar** play this staircase – which is in fact a **sea-powered organ.**

INSTRUMENTAL
ODDITIES

HYDRAULOPHONE

An **instrument** that looks a bit like a garden sprinkler, the **hydraulophone** is played by putting your fingers over **jets of water.** Some have even been added to **hot tubs!**

WILLIAM TELL ROAD

In California, USA, there is a **road** that is designed to play composer **Rossini's 'William Tell Overture'** as you drive down it, via a series of grooves in the **road's surface.**

ZEUSAPHONE

An **instrument** that takes using **electricity** to make sound to the next level, the **Zeusaphone** uses a lightning-making **Tesla coil** to create music.

FIRE ORGAN

The **pyrophone** is a strange organ, invented in the **19th century,** that uses fiery **hydrogen explosions** to create sounds.

OCTOBASS

The **octobass** is the world's **largest double bass.** It's so big that it needs a **special** platform and **foot pedals** to be able to play it.

DID YOU KNOW?

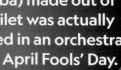

A loophonium (a type of brass instrument, similar to a tuba) made out of a toilet was actually played in an orchestra – on April Fools' Day.

UNUSUAL ART

Pincher Calls

Spanish artist Salvador Dali is well-known for crafting surrealist art. One of his strangest pieces was the fusion of a lobster and a telephone!

3D Paintings

In Chiang Mai, Thailand, there is a 3D art museum where visitors can interact and mingle with the mindboggling masterpieces.

Totally **WEIRD!**

Sometimes art can really move a mountain. Or a sand dune. In 2002, artist Francis Alÿs gathered 500 volunteers at a sand dune outside of Peru's capital city, Lima, and gave them each a shovel. The art project he directed was to get them to move the massive dune 10 centimetres from its original spot.

On Your Bikes

Ai Weiwei is an artist who really likes bicycles. His sculptures feature thousands of bicycles stacked together to make strange geometric patterns, but don't think about taking one for a ride – the artist makes sure to remove the seats and the pedals to make the bikes seem more abstract.

Flying Cat

Dutch artist Bart Jansen honoured his cat's life by transforming it into a feline drone. The cat, called Orville, loved birds so Jansen believed this would turn Orville into an aviator, just like birds and his namesake, Orville Wright.

See-Saw Through the Wall

In 2019, a professor of architecture and a professor of design decided to install pink see-saws right through the slats of the US–Mexico border fence. Although the see-saws were only up for 40 minutes, children on both sides of the border enjoyed the temporary playground.

The **longest song** to be released so far is called 'The Rise and Fall of Bossanova' by Michael J. Bostwick's **PC III** project. If you can handle the listening experience, it takes over **13 hours from start to finish.**

The longest song to reach number 1 in the **UK charts** is 'All Around the World' by Oasis, which is short by comparison – clocking in at just over **9.5 minutes.**

In the **USA,** the longest song to reach number 1 is **'American Pie'** by singer-songwriter Don McLean. It is a relatively brief at 8 minutes, 34 seconds long.

The **longest piece of music** ever written is called 'As Slow As Possible', written by composer John Cage. A performance **started in 2001,** with a 17-month pause, in **St Burchardi Church,** Halberstadt, **Germany.** It is not due to finish until the year **2640** – making it a 639-year-long piece of music.

The organ at St Burchardi Church.

FUN FESTIVALS

KUKUR TIHAR

An annual Hindu festival in Nepal is dedicated to thanking dogs for their friendship towards humans. The festival also celebrates cows and crows. Kukur Tihar is also held in Mexico and Australia. During the festival dogs are decorated with garlands of flowers and coloured powder marks, called tika, on each dog's forehead.

TWIN TOWN

The people of Igbo-Ora in Nigeria produce a lot of twins. The country has the world's highest birth-rate of twins and in Igbo-Ora there is hardly a family that doesn't have a set of twins. Each year, the town holds a festival that celebrates their double bundles of joy.

BRINGING IN SUMMER WITH A BANG

Each spring, in Zurich, Switzerland, there is a festival that marks the end of winter by filling the head of a snowman figure – called the Böögg – with fireworks. According to local legend, the quicker the Böögg's head explodes, the better the summer that year will be.

A MUSIC FESTIVAL THAT MAKES A SPLASH

In Florida, USA, a music festival is held every year – 6 metres underwater! The festival raises awareness of the coral reef to ensure that people understand how important they are for the world's environment, but it is also a chance to dress up and enjoy music piped into the reef via underwater speakers.

ALASKAN MOOSE POO

At the Moose Dropping festival in Talkeetna, Alaska, people choose a dried bit of Moose poo that has been lacquered and numbered, which is then dropped from a helicopter or a hot air balloon on to a target on the ground. The person with the poo that lands closest to the target wins a prize.

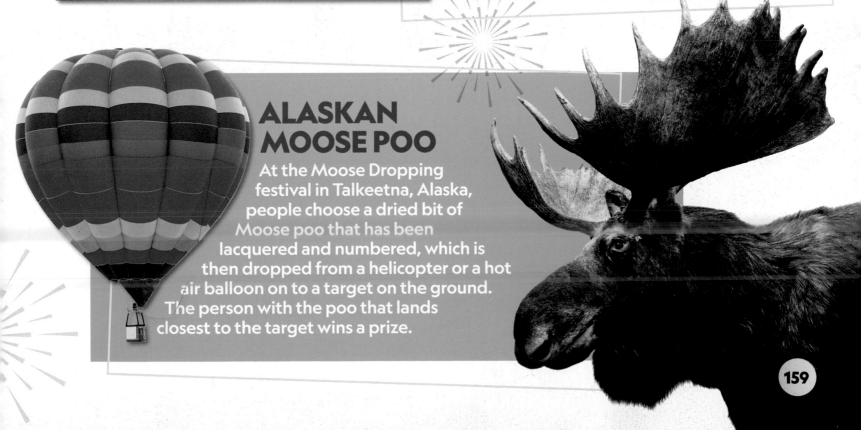

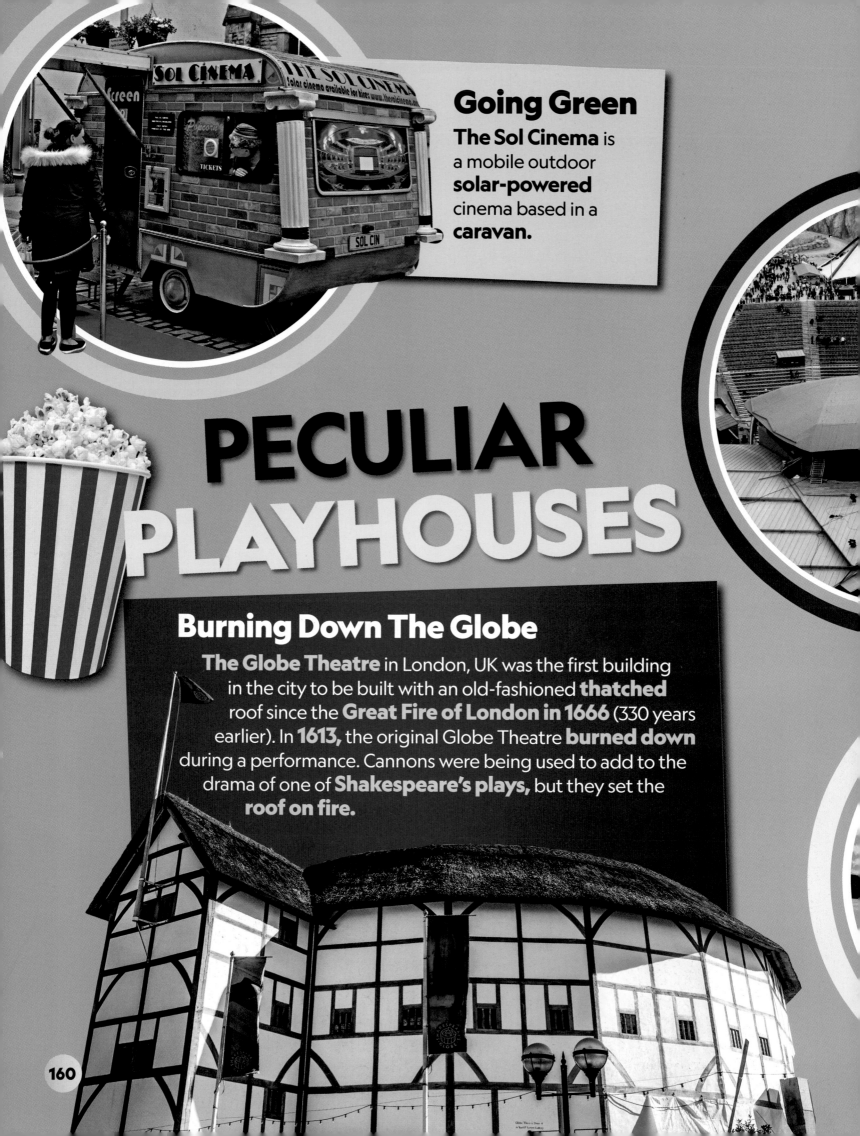

Going Green

The Sol Cinema is a mobile outdoor **solar-powered** cinema based in a **caravan.**

PECULIAR PLAYHOUSES

Burning Down The Globe

The Globe Theatre in London, UK was the first building in the city to be built with an old-fashioned **thatched** roof since the **Great Fire of London in 1666** (330 years earlier). In **1613,** the original Globe Theatre **burned down** during a performance. Cannons were being used to add to the drama of one of **Shakespeare's plays,** but they set the **roof on fire.**

Rocking out

Dalhalla is a theatre and concert venue situated in an **old limestone quarry,** in central **Sweden.**

Mime Time

Four hundred and twenty mimes – actors who use **body language** instead of speaking – were employed by the **Mayor** of **Bogota, Colombia,** to copy the movements of pedestrians who didn't follow the rules of **crossing the road.** They also **mocked people** who drove **recklessly.**

Tiny Toilet Humour

There is a **mini theatre** in Great Malvern, UK, that is a converted **Victorian public toilet.** Bought in 1997 by **puppeteer Dennis Neale,** the **tiny stone building** seats only **12 people.**

CHECK MATE

Chess is a strategy game in which two armies take turns moving across a checkerboard to capture the opposing player's king. It is thought to have originated in India around 1,500 years ago. While it is simple to learn the different moves that the pieces can make, it can take a lifetime to master. The youngest player to become a chess grandmaster, Sergey Karjakin, was only 12 years old when he earned the title, having started learning the game when he was five.

The largest chess set in the world is in Canada. The board is over 5 metres square and the king stands more than 1 metre tall. At the other end of the scale, a Turkish sculptor created a micro chess set that is about as big as a fingernail!

Sergey Karjakin

The game has over 2,000 different variations, including three-player chess (played on a hexagonal board) and 'anti-king' chess (where each player has an additional king that can only take its own pieces and is in check when not being attacked).

Chess has been played in lots of strange places – in 1970, cosmonauts in space played on a special chessboard against opponents back on Earth. There is even a World Championship in diving chess – there is special chess set at the bottom of a chest-deep pool and players take turns diving down to make their move. People have also taken to playing chess on rollercoasters and water-flumes! One of the strangest ways to play chess is perhaps the sport of chess boxing. Competitors play chess for 4 minutes, then box each other for 3 minutes. After a quick rest, they then carry on the game of chess. If they can!

Gardener's WORLD

The Garden of Cosmic Speculation

Located in Scotland and only open to the public once every year, the Garden of Cosmic Speculation mixes twisted geometric patterns and mind-bending physics into a beautiful green landscape. Visitors can go on a 'Quark Walk' and explore a swirling chessboard 'black hole'.

The Longest Maze in the World

The longest maze in the world is in China, it is shaped like an elk, and is nearly 9.5 kilometres long. Which means that the ten rest-spots dotted around the maze come in very handy when trying to find your way through!

Giants in the Hillside

The Cerne Abbas Giant is a 180-foot naked outline of a man carved into the side of a hill in Dorset, England. In 2007, he was joined by a similarly huge outline of Homer Simpson, holding a doughnut. Luckily, the people who had added Homer Simpson used materials that melted away in the rain.

A Guitar Made of Trees

In Argentina, a farmer planted a forest of over 7,000 cypress and eucalyptus trees in the shape of a guitar. The guitar-shaped forest was made as a memorial to the farmer's wife who died in 1977.

The Big Pink Bunny

There is a giant pink bunny on a hillside in Italy. The 60-metre-long rabbit was knitted by a group of artists who used waterproof wool. They packed the enormous (and slightly creepy looking) bunny with straw and they encourage visitors to climb on the giant rabbit and take naps there.

Grub's UP!

CHAPTER **10**

A **MAN** once PUSHED a **BRUSSELS SPROUT** to the top of MOUNT SNOWDON **USING** his NOSE.

Jump to page 177 for more facts on super sprouts!

Glorious GUM!

Gum Painter

Ben Wilson is an English artist who turns discarded chewing gum into art. Ben transforms the gum, which is stuck to pavements, by adding a lick of paint! He has created over 10,000 tiny artworks. As he is painting art onto litter, it isn't technically against the law.

Bubblegum Alley

There is a place in California called Bubblegum Alley – it has gum stuck there from passers-by and now has millions of pieces of chewed-up gum on the walls.

Forever Blowing Bubbles

Bubble gum was invented in 1928 by Walter Deimer who worked at a chewing gum factory – as an accountant!

Freaky Flavours

There are some very odd flavours of gum – including meatball, beef, turkey (with cranberry), bacon and even something called **'man smell'**!

No Gum Allowed

Selling chewing gum is banned in Singapore. You can only get chewing gum from the dentist or doctor in Singapore as it needs to be prescribed.

Oldest Gum

Chewing gum is a habit that humans have had for a long time. A 5,000-year-old bit of chewed gum – made from birch sap – was found in Finland, with toothmarks still visible.

Keep Chewing!

Around 100,000 tonnes of gum is chewed each year – that weighs around the same as 25,000 Indian elephants!

THE NATION'S FAVOURITE ...

FISH and CHIPS

Fish and chips used to come wrapped in old newspaper. Until the 1980s, this was perfectly normal; however, it has since been prohibited because it is unsafe for food to be contaminated by newspaper ink.

The world's oldest fish and chip shop can be found in West Yorkshire, United Kingdom. The premises have been serving the dish to customers since the 1860s.

A fish and chip shop in Glasgow, Scotland once sold over 12,000 portions in a single day!

In China, people like to sprinkle sugar over their fish and chips.

In Britain, approximately £1.2 billion is spent on fish and chips each year.

A survey of British people found that fish and chips were one of the nation's favourite smells, along with freshly baked bread and clean laundry.

Juicy Fruits

VITAMIN PEPPER

There is more vitamin C in a sweet pepper than there is in an orange.

BANANAS ARE BERRIES

Technically, a banana is a berry. Even weirder: a strawberry isn't a berry, its known as a pseudocarp or 'false fruit'. Berries have their seed on the inside of the fruit. Strawberries have their seeds on the outside of the fruit. **Tomatoes, avocados, pumpkins and watermelons** are all types of berry!

THE QUEEN OF FRUITS

The sweet and tangy mangosteen is known as 'The Queen of Fruits'. It is grown in southeast Asia and is the national fruit of Thailand. Legend says that Queen Victoria once offered a £100 reward to anyone who could bring her a mangosteen.

CHERRY COPTER

Did you know that cherries can be damaged from rainfall? So, after heavy rain, helicopters are used to blow dry cherry trees.

AN APPLE A DAY

There are over 7,500 types of apple. Eating a different type of apple every day, it would take you over 20 years to get through them all. Weirdly, if you planted the seeds of the apples you ate, you are unlikely to get trees that produced the same apples. They are likely to be totally different and might not taste very nice.

THE KING OF FRUITS

The durian, from southeast Asia, is known as 'The King of Fruits'. This large, thorn-covered fruit is also known for being so bad-smelling that it is banned from underground train systems in Singapore. The strong smells of the durian have been described as like rotten onions, vomit and pig poo!

Mystery Flavour Drinks

Anything (carbonated) and Whatever (non-carbonated) were the names of two drinks. Each came in various flavours (Anything had a mix of cola, apple, lemon and root beer; Whatever had different types of tea), but the cans didn't reveal what they were.

Drink Up

Totally WEIRD!

In Canada, adults can order a drink that is served with a mummified toe in it.

Cola and Submarines

Soft drink company Pepsi was once paid in submarines. In 1989, the Soviet Union government had purchased a lot of cola from Pepsi and so paid them with 17 submarines and three warships. Pepsi sold them for scrap.

Tasty Tuna

In South Korea there's a drink that is made using the fluid from the eyes of a tuna fish.

Slurping on Pizza

Brewers in the United Kingdom have developed a beer that tastes like pizza.

Poo Coffee

There is a type of coffee in which the coffee beans (below) have been eaten, partially digested and pooed out by palm civets, before being used to make the drink. Called kopi luwak, this coffee is one of the most expensive in the world – a single cup could cost you around £70! However, increased demand for this speciality drink has resulted in many palm civets being treated badly at coffee plantations, with them often having very poor living conditions.

Holiday SEASON

FESTIVE FEAST

In the USA over 40 million turkeys are eaten during the Thanksgiving holiday.

SALTED SHEEP HEAD

A traditional Norwegian dish usually eaten before Christmas, is sheep's head that has been smoked and steamed.

SOUTHERN FRIED CHRISTMAS

In Japan, it has become custom to eat Kentucky Fried Chicken on Christmas day.

A WEEK OF PANCAKES

In Russia, the end of winter is celebrated with Maslenitsa – a week-long festival that encourages people to eat blinis, which are Russian pancakes.

15,000 EGGS

An Easter festival in France involves an omelette being made by the Brotherhood of the Giant Omelette that uses over 15,000 eggs.

CHRISTMAS CATERPILLARS

Mopane 'worms' (actually caterpillars), are eaten in southern Africa around Christmas (because they are seasonal then). They are fried with tomato, onion and chili.

BRITAIN AND BRUSSELS

In the United Kingdom, brussels sprouts are a staple on the Christmas dinner plate. In fact, each year, British people eat more brussels sprouts per head than any other country in Europe.

SUPER
strawberries

Strawberries are the **ONLY FRUIT** in the world that have their **SEEDS** on the **OUTSIDE** and not the inside.

27 FEBRUARY is **NATIONAL STRAWBERRY DAY.**

The **AVERAGE** strawberry has around 200 **SEEDS.**

Strawberries contain **HIGH LEVELS** of **NITRATE** and can help increase **OXYGEN** flow to **MUSCLES** and improve **EXERCISE** performance. Nitrates are found **NATURALLY** in many fruits and vegetables.

CHINA is the WORLD'S BIGGEST GROWER of strawberries.

There is a **MUSEUM** in Wépion, **BELGIUM** that is dedicated to strawberries. The **'MUSÉE DE LA FRAISE'** tells the **HISTORY** of strawberry **PRODUCTION** in the region.

Strawberries belong to the **ROSE FAMILY.** Not only do they taste sweet, but they **SMELL SWEET** too.

In **ANCIENT ROME,** strawberries were believed to have **MEDICINAL PROPERTIES.** The fruit was used to treat ailments such as **SORE THROATS** and **STINKY BREATH.**

The state of **CALIFORNIA** is responsible for around 75% of the strawberries **GROWN** in the USA.

The human
BODY

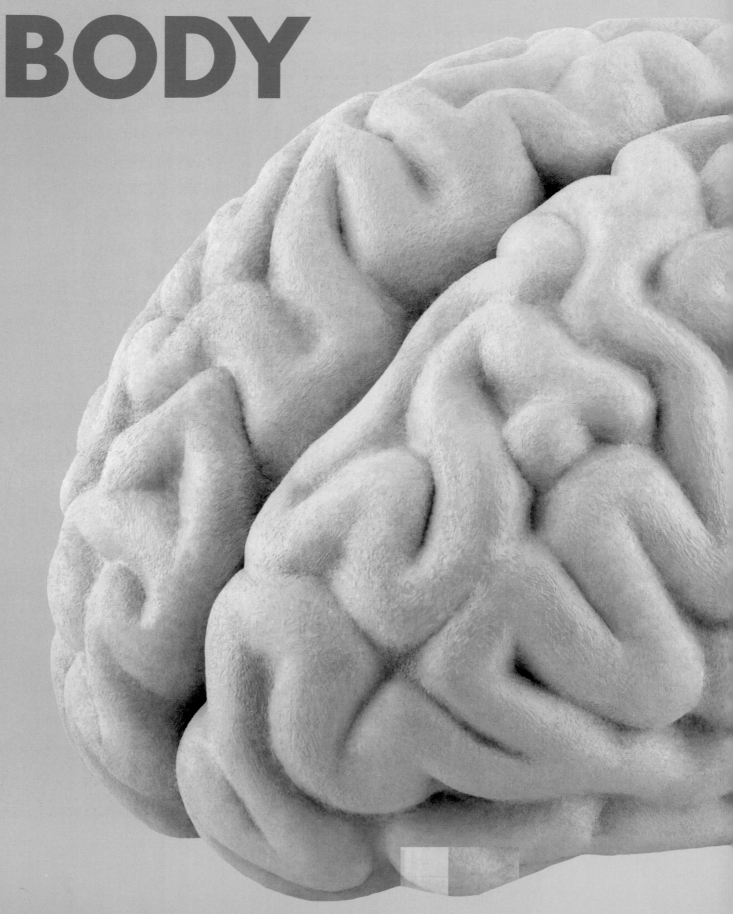

The **QUANTITY** of FOLDS and WIGGLES in the **SURFACE** indicates the COMPLEXITY of the BRAIN. **HUMANS,** MONKEYS and **DOLPHINS** all have brains with a lot of folds.

Pop to page 186 for more brain-based trivia.

BIG
BABIES

BABIES GROW

about 3 centimetres every month up to 6 months old.

After that, they grow around 1 centimetre per month until they are 1 year old. After this growth spurt, things slow down a bit. But what if babies kept growing at the same rate as when they were first born?

If a baby was born at 50 centimetres in length, by the age of 3-and-a-half, the baby would be 176 centimetres tall – the same height as a fully grown adult!

By age 18 they'd be nearly 7 metres tall – that's as tall as a Spinosaurus – one of the largest carnivores to have ever lived, or about as tall as a two-storey building!

Babies also start life with more bones than adults. When you're born, you have around 300 bones, which fuse together over time. Why? Because a baby needs to be more flexible to be able to grow, both in the womb and once they are born. Adults have 206 bones – so you 'lose' nearly 100 bones by the age of 25.

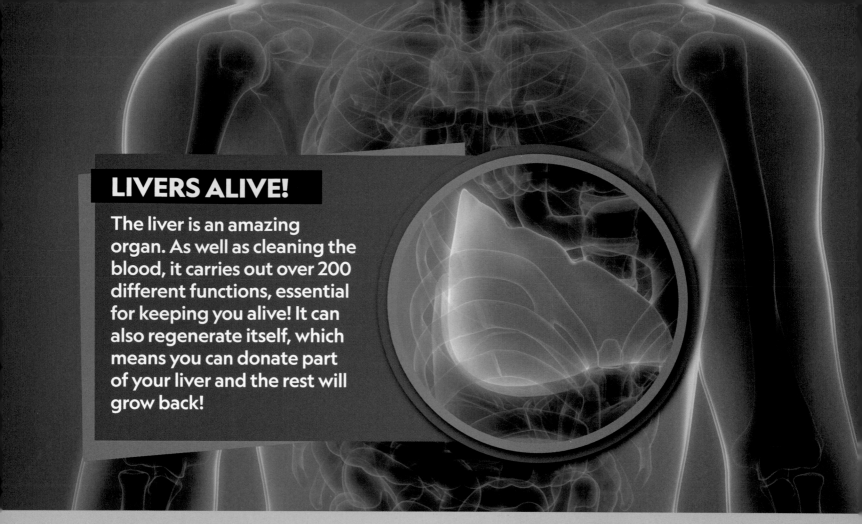

LIVERS ALIVE!

The liver is an amazing organ. As well as cleaning the blood, it carries out over 200 different functions, essential for keeping you alive! It can also regenerate itself, which means you can donate part of your liver and the rest will grow back!

ORGAN
Players

THE WAY OF 'ALL FLESH'

The pancreas is an organ that sits between your stomach and your intestines. The pancreas produces enzymes, which help humans digest food. If things go wrong and the enzymes start acting before they leave the pancreas, it can actually start to digest itself!

LESS HUMAN THAN HUMAN?

Human beings are made of human stuff, right? Well, there are also a lot of other things that live in and on your body. About half of all the cells in your body are not, strictly speaking, *you*. For instance, there are tiny little mites, called Demodex mites (right), that live at the base of your eyelashes and eat dead skin cells.

YOU TUBES

Your body is a bag of tubes – tubes that go from your nose to your lungs, tubes that go from your ears to inside your head, and tubes that carry food from your mouth to your bum (over 9 metres of them). There are also tubes that transport your blood all around your body (which, if you could lay them all out, would stretch over 100,000 kilometres – long enough to go around the Earth two and a half times)!

Bacteria IN YOUR Bum

There are bacteria living in your bum. In fact, there are lots of them! Hundreds of different species of bacteria live in your colon, which is the last stop in the digestive system before you poo.

These Facts will BL💥W your Brain

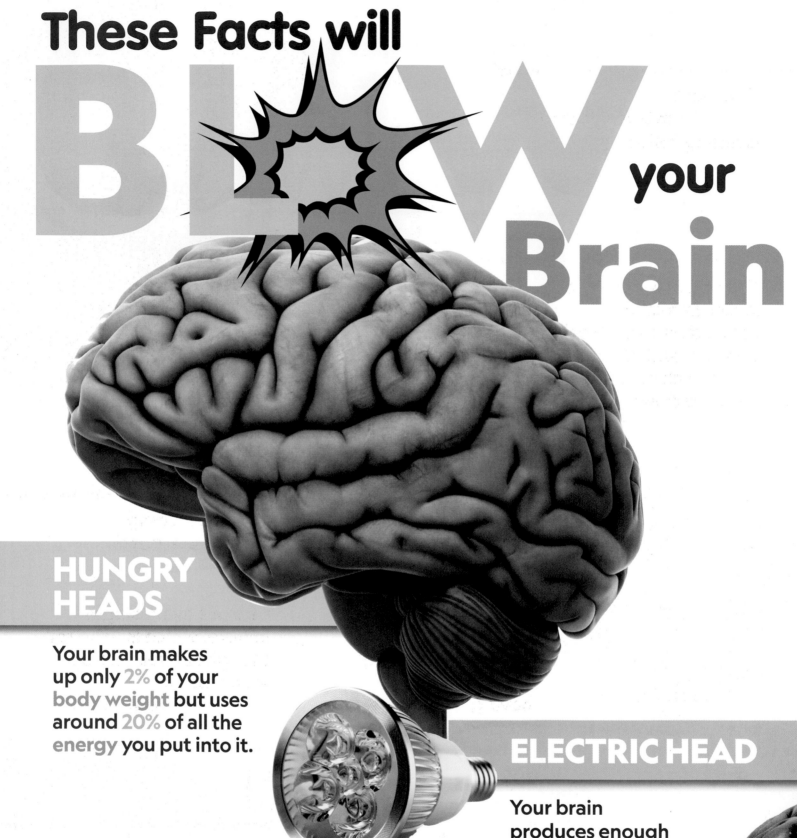

HUNGRY HEADS

Your brain makes up only 2% of your body weight but uses around 20% of all the energy you put into it.

ELECTRIC HEAD

Your brain produces enough electricity to power a small LED light.

FAT BRAINS

Your brain is the fattest organ in the body. Over half of the brain (60%) is made of fat, which help it to function properly.

Thinking Machine

The most complex structure in the universe is hiding inside your skull –your brain!

Threads and Glue

Your brain is made up of structures called neurons, connected to each other by threads, and gluey cells called glia, which help protect and develop them.

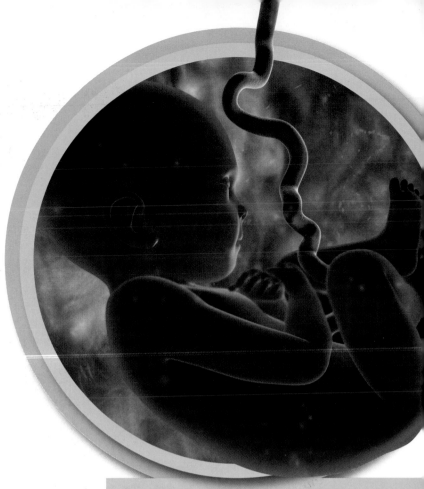

NO PAIN BRAIN

Brains have no nerve endings that detect pain, which means that people can actually be awake while having brain surgery.

BUILDING BLOCKS

As a developing foetus, you make around

250,000

neurons every single minute, which is food for thought as you end up with around 86 billion neurons in your brain.

A Brain of Two Halves

Your brain is split into two halves (called hemispheres). Amazingly, the remaining hemisphere can sometimes take over the functions of the other half if it has been removed for surgery!

THE NEED FOR SPEED

The messages sent by the brain travel at super high speeds – faster than a Formula 1 car!

Face Facts

FASTEST MUSCLE

The fastest muscles in the human body are found around the eyelid! These are the muscles that make you blink. A blink lasts around one-tenth of a second. And, each day, the average person blinks around 20,000 times. Some scientists think we have a tiny rest while we blink, which helps us to focus.

THE 5, 6, 7, 8 9 SENSES...

Humans have more than the five senses of sight, hearing, touch, taste and smell. For instance, what about your sense of balance? Or your sense of space? Scientists agree that there are at least 9 senses. Some think there are over 20 senses!

BITING POWER

One of the strongest muscles in your body is in your face – it is called the masseter muscle and is the one that lets you chew on things. Scientists have discovered that chewing your food improves the health of the mouth and its ability to fight off infection.

A **NOSE** FOR DISEASE

A woman claimed to be able to smell a disease, so scientists tested her – they gave her 12 T-shirts to sniff. Six of the T-shirts were from people who had the disease, six weren't. The woman correctly identified the six that had the disease but also chose one from the other group. Eight months later, the owner of the seventh T-shirt was unfortunately diagnosed with the illness.

DON'T WORRY,
BE HAPPY

Smiling actually reduces the amount of pain you feel. Smiling is also linked to being healthier in general, whether it's a genuine smile or just an act, stress can be reduced.

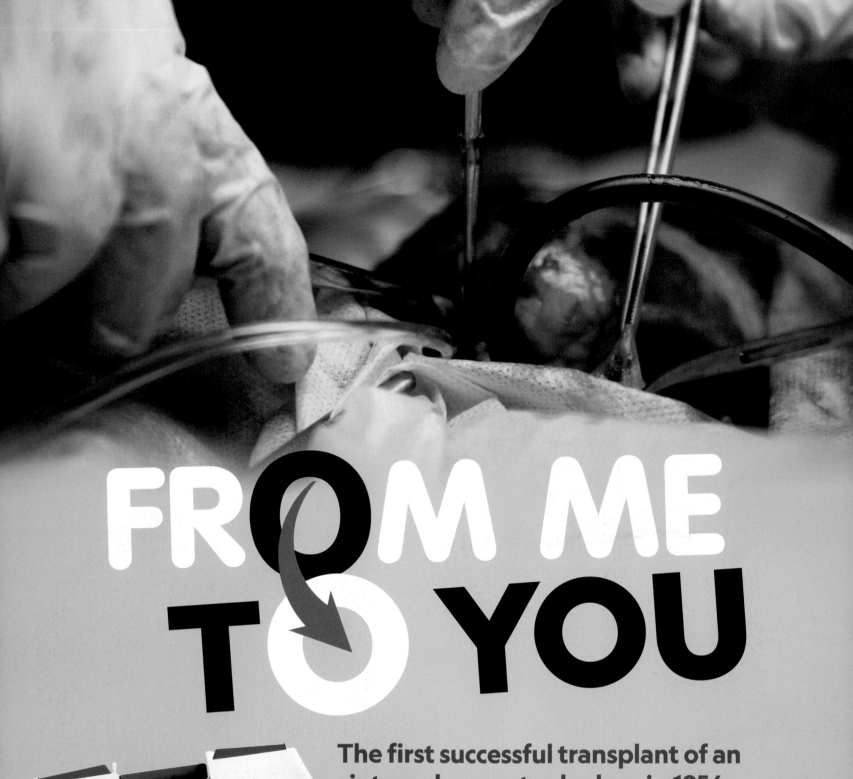

FR**O**M ME T**O** YOU

HUMAN ORGAN

The first successful transplant of an internal organ took place in 1954 – that's less than 100 years ago.

All previous attempts at transplanting had failed because the patient's body would always reject the organ. Their body thought the new organ was an impostor and attacked it, which didn't help them out.

The organ transplanted was a kidney. The two people involved were identical twins, which made things a lot easier. The transplant was a success and extended the life of the recipient for a further eight years.

The first ever heart transplant took place in the 1960s in South Africa. The heart of a young woman who had died in a car accident was successfully transplanted into the chest of a grocer in his fifties.

FAST FACTS

In the United Kingdom, there are approximately 5,000 people waiting for an organ transplant.

It is possible to donate some organs while you are still alive, such as your kidney or part of your liver.

When donating an eye, the whole eye is not transplanted – it is usually the cornea.

SKIN
DEEP

LIGHT SKIN IS NEW

Humans only developed lighter-toned skin about 8,000 years ago. It is thought it developed as people moved further away from the tropics to areas with lower rates of UV radiation.

Totally WEIRD!

Skin accounts for approximately 16% of a human's total body weight.

FRECKLE FACTS

Nobody is born with freckles. They are a reaction to sunlight, which babies don't get until after they are born!

THICK and THIN

The thinnest skin on your body is on your eyelids (about 0.05 millimetres). The thickest skin is on the soles of your feet (about 1.5 millimetres thick).

BIGGEST PROTECTOR

Skin is the largest organ – and every 28 days all of your outermost skin is renewed.

A METALLIC SMELL?

Humans can't actually smell metal. What we smell is the reaction of the metal we touch with the oils in our skin.

HUMAN ZEBRAS?

Human skin is actually stripey. The stripes are very faint and can only be seen under ultraviolet light.

AN ICY CANVAS

The oldest known tattoo was discovered on a body found preserved in ice. The body is known as Otzi and he lived over 5,000 years ago. He has over 60 tattoos!

Gruesomely
GROSS

NAKED MOLE RATS practise 'COPROPHAGY'. This means they **EAT** their own FAECES which helps **MAXIMISE** the NUTRIENTS they **CONSUME.**

Scurry to page 211 to read more gross facts about naked mole rats.

POO!

WHITE WASTE

The pristine, white sandy beaches found in the Maldives and Hawaii are made from parrotfish waste!

POO DIVE

In Australia, some people work as professional poo divers – they dive into human sewage to fix and maintain the machines that process the poo. This is because, in Australia, bacteria, not chemicals, are used to break the sewage down. This leads to more breakdowns in the machinery, which leads to the need for heroic poo divers.

SLOTHS
On average, sloths only poo once a week.

POO TIME

SUN	MON	TUE	WED	THU	FRI	SAT
23			1	2	3	4	5
6	7	8	9	10	11	12
13	14	15	16	17	18	19
20	21	22	23	24	25	26
27	28	29	30			

THAT'S NOT A KNIFE
Peter Freuchen was an arctic explorer. On an expedition to Greenland in 1926, he got trapped in snow during a blizzard, which then hardened to ice. He used a frozen bit of his own poo to dig himself out. He made it back to camp but had to amputate some of his toes as they had become frostbitten in the cold.

A VERY SMELLY FATE
In 1184, the King Heinrich VI of Germany organised a meeting of noble people from across Europe to resolve a dispute. About 60 noblemen turned up at a church in Germany to help with the talks. As the meeting went on, the combined weight of all the noblemen caused the floor to collapse. Around 60 people fell through the floor into the cellar, which was used as a latrine – basically a big open toilet. And all 60 of them ended up drowning in human waste!

A STINKY CITY
In London, 1858 was known as the Year of the Stink. Politicians in the Houses of Parliament couldn't work as the nearby River Thames was full of sewage and household and industrial gunk. The smell was overpoweringly awful. Although scientists had proven that thousands of Londoners had died through drinking dirty water, it was the stench from the river that finally convinced the leaders of the country that London needed a proper sewer system.

BOGEY FACTS

Pick and Eat

Mucophagy is the scientific name for picking your nose and eating it.

Bogey count

A study found that **91%** of respondents picked their nose on a daily basis. If that percentage was applied to the world population, it would mean almost **7 billion people** are **picking, rolling** and **flicking** every day!

198

Mucus Galore

Each human produces 1–1.5 litres of mucus every day but we swallow most of it. In a year, it could fill over three bathtubs!

Picking with Pals

'Pass the Booger' is a card game that has participants trying to collect six 'booger cards' while avoiding the 'booger' itself. 'PoPeln' is another game where people pick plastic noses to try and find as many bogeys as possible.

Signed, Sneezed, Delivered

Actress Scarlett Johansson once sold a handkerchief she'd sneezed into to raise money for charity. The signed hankie sold for over $5,000.

Whale Snot

Collecting whale-snot is an actual job. Scientists have spent years gathering mucus from the blowholes of Beluga whales to test the stress levels of these ocean-dwelling mammals.

199

FOUL FOOD

CHOPPING BOARD

Your chopping board has more **germs** than your **toilet seat.** A study concluded that a kitchen chopping board has over **20,000 bacteria** per square centimetre.

JELLYBEAN SHINE

Jellybeans are shiny because they are coated in **shellac,** which is made from a substance secreted by the **lac beetle.** Humans have been using it for over **3,000 years!**

MOULDY FOOD FOR THOUGHT

In the USA, the Food and Drug Administration sets maximum levels of **hairs, maggots and other contaminants** in a whole range of foodstuffs. For example, a maximum of two rodent hairs in 50 grams of ground pepper is acceptable.

SURSTRÖMMING

Suströmming is a delicacy from Sweden and is one of the **stinkiest foods in the world.** It contains whole, **fermented herring** and has been **banned** from being brought on board aeroplanes in many different countries.

SCRUMPTIOUS SNAILS

Escargots is a dish from **France** that consists of edible **snails** which are usually cooked in **garlic butter** and stock. It's not just France where escargots is enjoyed, people across Europe and northern Africa are partial to the dish.

A FOUL FROMAGE

Vieux Boulogne is a cheese from northern France. A panel crowned this cheese the **whiffiest** of the 15 cheeses being tested. A second assessment by an electronic nose also confirmed Vieux Boulogne as the **stinkiest**. Its foul smell comes from **the rind** which is **washed in beer.**

Medical
PROCEDURES

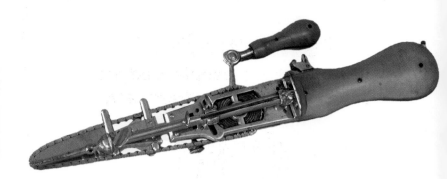

Chainsaws
The precursor to the chainsaw – now commonly used to cut down trees – was originally designed by **two Scottish surgeons** to assist with **childbirth!**

Leeches
For thousands of years, doctors used to think that **bloodletting** (removing some of the patient's blood) would help to cure many diseases. To do this they used **bloodsucking leeches,** sometimes removing over **half of a patient's blood!**

Dead Mouse
In **Ancient Egypt,** if you were complaining of **toothache,** it may have been treated by **cutting a mouse in half and putting the bloody part** on your sore gums!

Pearly Whites?

In **Roman times,** people used jars of **old pee to whiten their teeth.**

Hole in the Head

Trepanning is the name for perhaps the oldest known surgical procedure. It involves **drilling a hole in someone's head** to relieve pressure on the brain. Archaeologists have found **skulls** up to **8,000 years old** with **trepanning holes** from all across the world!

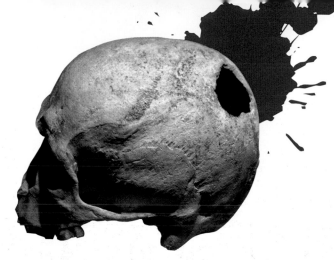

Maggot Therapy

Maggots are being used in modern **medical treatments.** Specially bred, and **sterile,** maggots are placed in a mesh; they are then put on to a **patient's wound** where they clean it by **eating infected** and **dead tissue** and **bacteria.**

No More Accidents!

In the 1st century AD, one suggested treatment to stop children **wetting the bed** was to **feed them a mouse!**

Totally WEIRD!

In the 18th century, one cure for coughing and a sore throat involved mixing dried dog poo with honey.

FAIRY TALES and FOLKLORE

Some of the world's most famous children's fairy stories have grisly origins. Some versions had much more death and violence than the ones that we know now.

⚠ WARNING – READING THIS MIGHT CHANGE YOUR VIEW OF SOME OF YOUR FAVOURITE CLASSIC STORIES.

In one version of **Goldilocks and the Three Bears**, the little girl with the golden hair and appetite for others' porridge, jumps through the bedroom window when she's discovered by the bear family – injuring herself in the process.

In the Brothers Grimm **Cinderella** story, one ugly sister cuts of her toes to make the slipper fit, while the other sister cuts off her heel.

There are many different versions of **Little Red Riding Hood**. In some, the wolf is actually a werewolf; in others, Red Riding Hood is eaten by the wolf.

In **Spanish culture**, the **tooth fairy** is a tooth mouse! In **Norway** there are tales of **tooth trolls** who live in the teeth of a boy. The purpose of the story is to encourage proper dental hygiene in children.

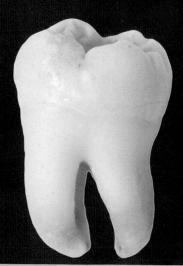

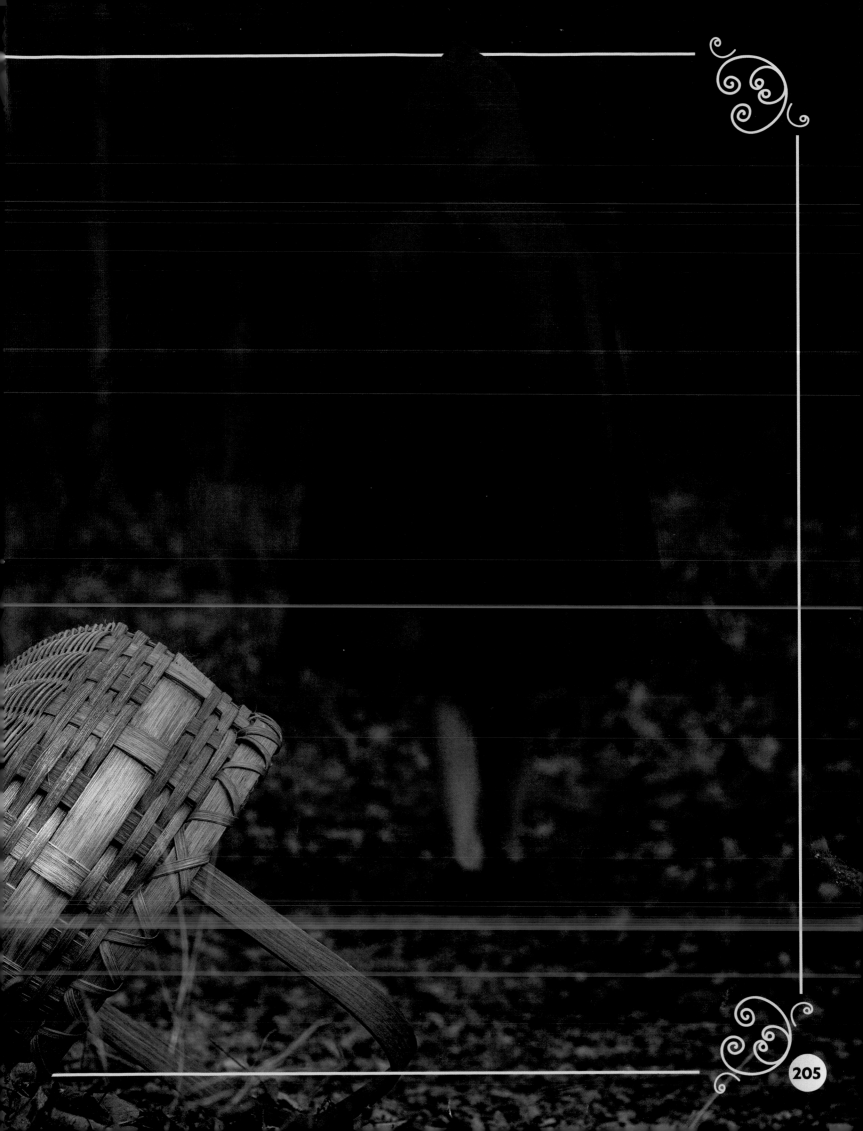

TANNER

The leather industry in the **18th and 19th centuries** created a lot of gross jobs, none more disgusting than that of a **tanner**. These were people who prepared and preserved the **skins of animals**. This involved soaking the skins in **lime** then scrubbing the **hair and fat** off the skins by hand. The skins would then be softened up by soaking them in a mixture of water and **dog, pig** or **chicken poo**!

ODD JOBS

WEE COLLECTORS

Scientists look at samples of **orangutan urine** to study factors that affect the animal's reproduction.

Totally **WEIRD!**

In Victorian Britain, the growth of industries brought people to cities, and with them, rats. Millions of rats. **Rat catchers** would rub sweet-smelling oils into their skin and clothes to attract rats, which they would catch by hand.

DOG'S BREAKFAST

Believe it or not, there is a job that involves testing dog and cat food. Someone has to check for consistency, texture, smell and taste.

FARTING AROUND

'Fart-smeller' is a real job. In China, people are paid to smell farts as a way of helping to detect and diagnose illnesses.

GUT SOUNDS

For centuries, instruments such as violins, cellos and guitars had strings made from 'catgut'. This was not the guts of a cat, but it was guts—the intestines from sheep, goats, cows or donkeys. The guts are cleaned by hand, stretched and then wound into strings.

all about YOU

Tummy Blush

When your **cheeks blush** the lining of your stomach also blushes!

Toilet Time

Over the course of your whole life, you'll spend around **a year sitting on the toilet.** And each year, you produce nearly 150 kilograms of poo — the same weight as a male **giant panda.**

Pooping Gold

There are traces of metals including copper, silver and gold in your poo. This comes from food, drink and medicine that is consumed. Scientists calculated that in one year, a million people could be **pooping out** around $13 million in precious metals!

Smelly Belly

The average person has **67 different types of bacteria** living in their belly button! Mozzarella was once made out of the **belly button bacteria** from Professor Green. The cheese was then displayed at the V&A Museum in London.

Totally WEIRD!

Humans fart around 5 – 15 times per day. During the period of the Samurai in Japan, farting competitions were held – the winner was the person who farted the loudest and longest.

Meibum

Meibum is the name of the stuff that you might **wipe out of your eyes** after a long night's sleep. This whitish gunk is actually very important. At normal body temperature, it is a clear liquid and coats the eyes to **stop tears** evaporating or dribbling down your face.

Fulmar

The fulmar is a seabird, similar to an albatross, that you would not want to annoy. When threatened, the fulmar sprays a stinky oily fishy vomit at its attacker. Fulmars also feed their young with regurgitated fish.

GROSS CREATURES

Frog Tummy

Frogs can't vomit. When they eat something that they shouldn't have, they flip their whole stomach inside out through their mouth and clean off their stomach using their arms. They then swallow their stomach back down. Sea cucumbers are even grosser – when threatened, these strange animals eject their intestines out of their bum or mouth to confuse and distract any nearby predator. They then regenerate their intestines within a few days.

Lampreys

After they are born, some species of lampreys (eel-like fish) bury themselves in the riverbed for up to seven years. When they come out, they have mouths lined with rings of vicious teeth. They even have teeth on their tongue. Lampreys use their teeth to attach to their food: other fish and marine mammals, and drain their bodily fluid.

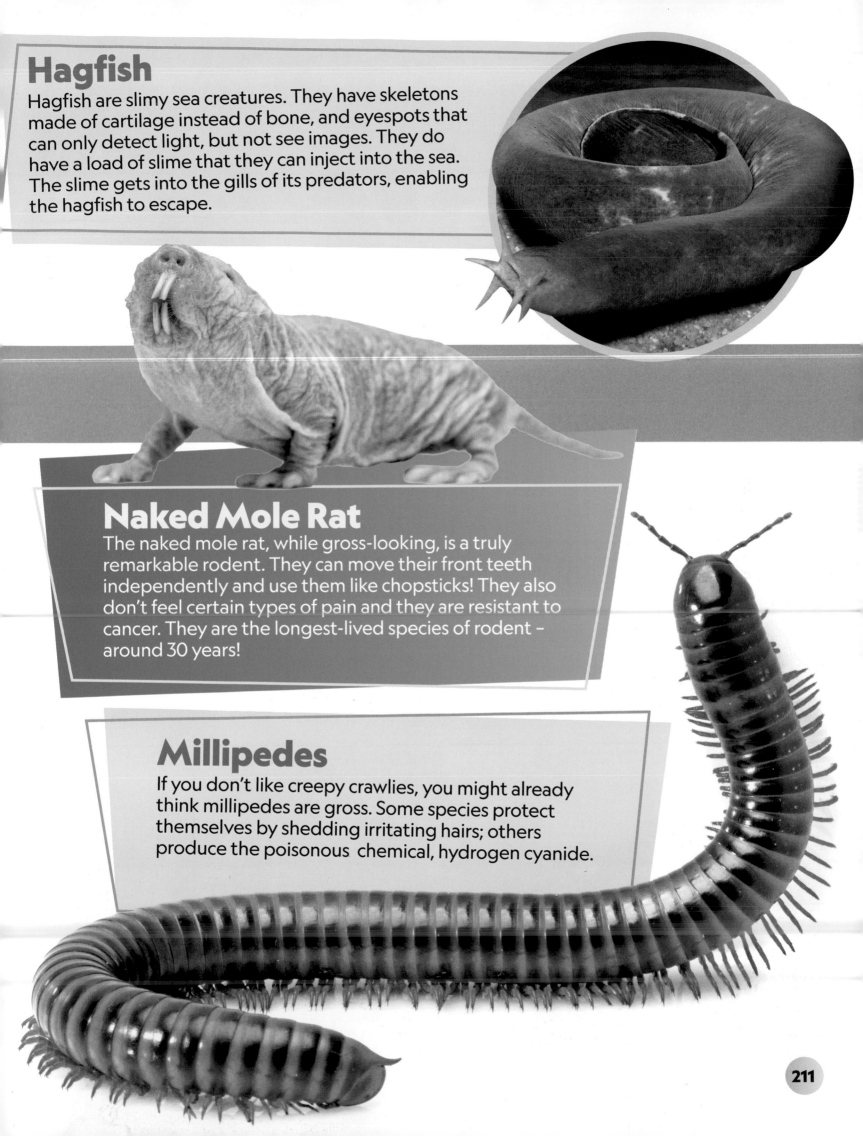

Hagfish

Hagfish are slimy sea creatures. They have skeletons made of cartilage instead of bone, and eyespots that can only detect light, but not see images. They do have a load of slime that they can inject into the sea. The slime gets into the gills of its predators, enabling the hagfish to escape.

Naked Mole Rat

The naked mole rat, while gross-looking, is a truly remarkable rodent. They can move their front teeth independently and use them like chopsticks! They also don't feel certain types of pain and they are resistant to cancer. They are the longest-lived species of rodent – around 30 years!

Millipedes

If you don't like creepy crawlies, you might already think millipedes are gross. Some species protect themselves by shedding irritating hairs; others produce the poisonous chemical, hydrogen cyanide.

FEAR and DISGUST

MOST HUMANS TEND TO BE DISGUSTED BY THE SMELLS OF THINGS THAT ARE ROTTEN. BUT WHY?

Scientists think that it is perhaps to stop us from **eating** something that might be **poisonous** or something that could pass on a disease. So sour odours, such as the smell of **gone-off milk** might make us think of things that are **rotten** or **infested** with **dangerous germs** and warn us to **stay away**.

People unfortunate enough to suffer from **Cacosmia** think everything **smells horrible.** Even a bunch of **roses** might smell like **rotten fish** to them.

Do you find **bedbugs** disgusting? Bedbugs are **parasites** (creatures that feed off other living creatures), and they suck blood. Mostly **human blood. Ticks** also feed on blood, filling up **balloon-like sacks** on their back. When one species of tick from Australia **bites** into its host, it releases a **toxin,** which **causes** a **paralysis** that sometimes leads to **death.**

A female tick feeding on a human.

Totally **WEIRD!**

The Titan Arum's flowering section can grow up to 3 metres high. It rarely flowers, and when it does, the flower emits a stench of rotting flesh, hence its nickname – the Corpse Flower.

Everything on the
ENVIRONMENT

AVOCADOS are being used to CREATE an ENVIRONMENTALLY FRIENDLY material called 'AVOPLAST'.

Turn to page 225 to see how avocados are helping the environment.

CHAPTER 13

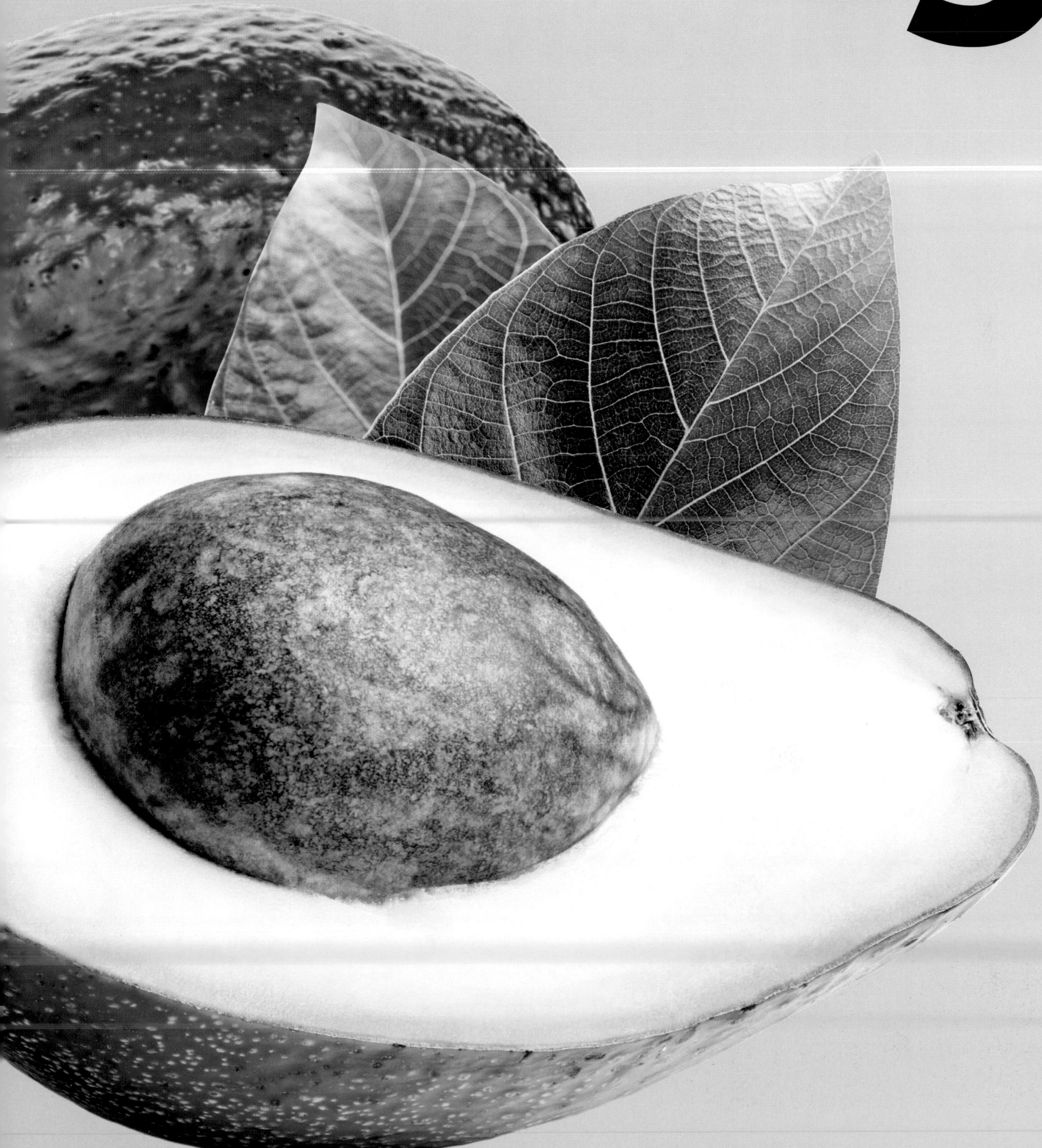

Cruisin' for Pollutin'

CRUISES can be popular holidays – almost **30 million people** went on a cruise holiday in 2019 – but they come with a cost to the environment.

In 2015, it was reported that one cruise ship at sea would emit more sulphur dioxide than 13 million cars. From January 2020, cruise ships were required to use cleaner fuels but it is still estimated that Europe's cruise ships will together emit over six times as much sulphur dioxide each year as all of the Europe's 260 million cars. And that's not all! A large cruise ship is basically like a floating city, which means a lot of other types of pollution – including noise pollution from the engines and the entertainment centres such as on-board cinemas and nightclubs.

A cruise ship carrying around 7,000 people generates around 1 million litres of human sewage and 4.5 litres of dirty water every week. This would be enough liquid to fill two Olympic-size swimming pools! And, after passing through an on-board water treatment machine, all of it is dumped straight into the ocean. So, the next time you're on a cruise ship, think twice before you flush!

WE HAVE
ALTERNATIVES!

SUN POWERED

Tamil Nadu, in India, has a pretty remarkable solar power plant. The Kamuthi power station is so large that it can create enough electricity to power 150,000 homes! Covering 10 square kilometres, or around the same size as 38,000 tennis courts, the plant is made up of over 2.5 million solar panels.

WATERFALL POWER

The world's most powerful hydroelectric power station is the Three Gorges Dam in China (right). The reservoir is so big and heavy that it has actually slowed the rotation of the Earth!

THE WINDS OF CHANGE

Wind turbines harness the power of the wind to generate electricity. The largest wind turbines are truly massive: each blade is over 105 metres long – which is taller than Big Ben. Hywind Scotland is the United Kingdom's first wind farm that uses floating wind turbines. In 2021, it set a record for the most power output from an offshore wind farm.

ICELAND'S UNDERGROUND SECRET

Iceland (left) is an island that sits on the mid-Atlantic ridge – where two tectonic plates meet. This means it has lots of volcanoes and earthquakes, but it also means it has easy access to heat that is normally hidden deep underground. Nine out of 10 homes in Iceland get their heating and hot water this way, and over 85% of the country's power is generated using renewable sources.

P**O**LLUTED PLANET

Not New News

110 years ago, a newspaper reported that burning fossil fuels could be a problem for the environment. In 1912, the article reported that **1.8 billion tonnes** of coal were burned each year, leading to around **6.3 billion tonnes** of the greenhouse gas carbon dioxide (CO_2) being released into the atmosphere. Today, it is estimated that there are around **13 billion tonnes** (double the amount) of CO_2 emissions from coal.

Plasticky Situation

Humans produce over **300 million** tonnes of plastic each year. At least **8 million tonnes** of this ends up in the oceans. Although the oceans are very big, there is hardly any spot in the sea that has been unaffected: we have even found plastic waste at the bottom of the Mariana Trench, which at almost **11 kilometres deep,** is the deepest ocean trench in the world.

Drip, Drip, Drip...

Do you have a dripping tap in your home? Is there one at school? Or perhaps you might have spotted one elsewhere. Treat each of these dripping things with suspicion (and a new washer). A dripping tap that drips once a second wastes around **20 litres** of water every day, which is over **7,500 litres every year**. And that's just **one** dripping tap!

Pump Down The Volume!

Noise pollution can be very damaging – to humans and to other animals. Children who live near noisy airports or streets can suffer from hearing loss, as well as attention and memory problems. In the ocean, sonar devices that send out very loud pulses of sound can interfere with whales, dolphins and other sea creatures' ability to communicate, navigate, and find a mate.

ISLANDS OF ICE

Because of **rising temperatures**, ice sheets are **breaking up**. In 2008, an area **larger** than the size of the island of **Malta** broke off the **Wilkins Ice Sheet** in **Antarctica**.

Ice, Ice, Maybe

IF ALL THE ICE MELTED

If all of the ice in Antarctica melted, **sea levels** would rise by around **60 metres** – that's as much as 13 double-decker buses stacked on top of each other. It would also mean that Glasgow, Manchester and London would be **underwater cities!**

ONE COLD SHEET

The **Antarctic ice sheet** is the largest in the world – covering **14 million** square metres. It is also **2 kilometres** thick.

FROZEN FLUID

Ice sheets **cover** almost all of the southern continent of Antarctica. **99%** of the world's surface **fresh water** is **trapped in ice**.

REFLECTORS

The ice sheets of the world act like **mirrors**, reflecting the Sun's energy back into space. **Shrinking ice sheets** means more of the **Sun's energy** is absorbed by the earth and oceans speeding up **global warming**.

THE DRIEST PLACE ON EARTH

The Dry Valleys of Antarctica were tundra until about 14 million years ago when they became dry – now they are the driest place on the planet.

SEA GOES UP

Since 1880, sea levels have **risen** by about **23 centimetres**. On average, seal levels have risen **3.6 millimetres** a year during the 20th century. However, the rate of sea level rise is speeding up and sea levels rose **6.1 millimetres** between 2018 and 2019.

BLOOD WATER

There is a **waterfall** in Antarctica that looks like it is gushing with **blood**. The red is due to **iron** ore scraped from the lake bed by the glacier and flows out due to water that is **too salty** to freeze.

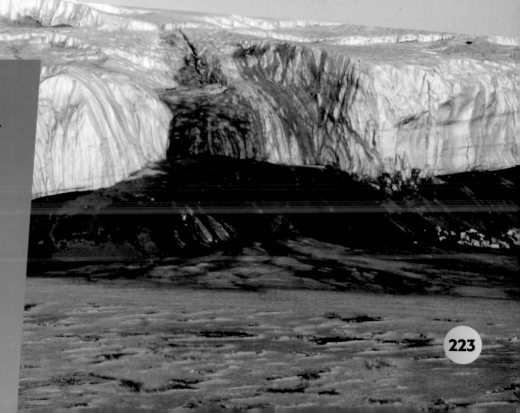

PLANTS and TREES

PLANT-IFUL PAKISTAN

The government of Pakistan have started a reforestation campaign with the aim of planting over 10 billion trees throughout the country. It is hoped that the initiative will reduce soil erosion and fight problems caused by climate change.

THE GREEN ENGINE

Ecosia is an online search engine that uses some of its profit to plant trees. For every 50 searches, a new tree is planted by the company. So far over 100 million trees have been planted around the world, helping to fight climate change and improving environmental stability.

A TREE A DAY...

A man in India has been planting a new tree every day for over 40 years. The colossal man-made forest is now larger than Central Park in New York and is home to an array of wildlife, including elephants, reptiles and birds.

AWESOME AVOCADOS

A company in Mexico has transformed avocado seeds into single-use cutlery and straws. Mexico is the world's largest producer of avocados, so seeds are in plentiful supply.

HUMAN POLLINATORS

Insects (and birds) have been pollinating flowers for millions of years. Pollinated plants are worth between £145 and £360 billion every year to the world economy. With a loss of insect species (such as bees, flies and midges) farmers are having to pollinate flowers by hand.

OUTSTANDING OSLO

Oslo, capital city of Norway, is committed to trying to reduce its impact on the environment. You can ride bicycles made from recycled materials, eat at a restaurant that uses left-over food that would otherwise be thrown away, and relax in a sauna that was built using driftwood!

Where Have All The Animals Gone?

Biodiversity describes the variety of different things that live on the planet. More biodiversity is good because it means that the planet is able to support lots of different forms of life. A report by the United Nations published in 2020 estimated that 1 million species are threatened with extinction. A quarter of all mammals are at risk of extinction. Until now, scientists have uncovered evidence of five other mass extinctions (times when nearly all of the life on the planet was wiped out). The last extinction was 65 million years ago and meant the end of the time of the dinosaurs. Some scientists are now arguing that we are living through a new mass extinction. This time, human beings, not asteroids, are the cause.

In the Asian countries of India, Pakistan, Nepal and Bhutan, vultures have been eating rotting carcasses for centuries. But a 99% drop in the vulture population is causing problems. In just 10 years, the Indian vulture suffered the quickest and most extreme population reduction in history. The culprit? A pain-killing drug which was given to livestock that the vultures then went on to eat. Eating meat that contained this drug led to kidney failure in the vultures. With fewer vultures to clear up the rotting carcasses of dead animals, the dog population grew, leading to a rise in diseases such as rabies.

Vultures are not the only species threatened with extinction. The black, Javan and Sumatran rhinos; the orangutan; three of the four species of gorillas; the Sunda tiger; the Sumatran elephant and the Amur leopard are just a few of over 7,000 species that are critically endangered.

By the NUMBERS

GIRAFFES are the **TALLEST ANIMALS** in the world. They can grow to **5.5 METRES TALL** – around the **SAME HEIGHT** as **THREE ADULT HUMANS!**

Trot over to page 236 for more animal number facts.

CHAPTER 14

Out for THE COUNT

11.57...
The number of **days** it would take to count to **1 million** if you counted one digit per second.

89...
The number of **days it actually took** someone to count to **1 million**, counting for **16 hours a day**.

6,670,903,752,021,072,936,960
The number of possible **different games** of **sudoku** in a standard **9 × 9 grid**.

Totally **WEIRD!**

A **googol** is a 1 with 100 zeroes after it. The word was invented by the nine-year old nephew of a mathematician in 1920. A googolplex is a 1 with a googol of zeroes after it. The Google search engine was named after the number (though it was mis-spelled).

1

Number of **websites** in 1991. Now there are over 1.8 billion – although only around **200 million** of these are 'active'.

50

The number of times you would have to **fold a piece of paper** for it to be thick enough to **reach to the Sun** (98 million miles).

7

The number of times you could **actually fold** a piece of A4 paper in half (you can't do it any more than that).

70

The number of **people** you need to have in a **room** for there to be a **99.9% chance** that **two** of them **share** the same **birthday**.

Countdown to
LAUNCH

The **SUN** has a mass over

300,000 times

greater than **planet Earth.**

It is responsible for over **99%** of our **SOLAR SYSTEM'S** total mass!

It takes **8 minutes** and **20 seconds** for **sunlight** to travel from the **SUN** to **EARTH.**

Ceres, **Makemake, Haumea,** Eris and **Pluto** make up the

5 DWARF PLANETS in our Solar System.

CERES

MAKEMAKE

HAUMEA

ERIS

PLUTO

In **2001,** Dennis Tito became the first **space tourist.** He visited the **INTERNATIONAL SPACE STATION** for **6 days** at a reported cost of **$20 million!**

THERE ARE MORE THAN **130 MILLION PIECES** OF **SPACE JUNK** IN ORBIT. TRAVELLING AT NEARLY

8 KILOMETRES PER SECOND.

THESE CAN CAUSE **SERIOUS DAMAGE!**

A BIT OF SPACE JUNK ONCE **CHIPPED THE WINDOW** OF THE **INTERNATIONAL SPACE STATION!**

Erno Rubik and the
MAGIC CUBE

Inventor Erno Rubik made the first ever 'Magic Cube' in 1974 out of bits of wood and paperclips. Now, more than 450 million Rubik's cubes have been sold, making it one of the most popular and recognisable puzzles in history!

27
Number of 'cubelets' that make up a Rubik's cube.

1.4 trillion years
The amount of time it would take to go through every possible combination of the puzzle if you turned it once a second. Even if you started at the Big Bang (13.7 billion years ago), you wouldn't be finished by now.

1 month
The length of time it took inventor Erno Rubik to solve his own puzzle.

20
The minimum number of moves required to solve the most complex configuration.

85,794
The number of Rubik's cubes used to create a mural of civil rights campaigner, Dr Martin Luther King, Jr.

2.022
The height, in metres, of the world's largest working Rubik's cube.

43 quintillion

The number of possible permutations of a standard Rubik's cube. That's 43 with 18 zeroes after it.

3.47 seconds

The quickest time for a standard Rubik's cube to be solved by a human (Yusheng Du in 2018). However, there is a robot that can solve a cube in only 0.38 seconds.

2,700

The weight (in kilograms) of the tongue of a blue whale. That's the same weight as an African forest elephant!

30

The length, in metres, of a blue whale – that's around the same length as a basketball court. The blue whale is not only the largest animal alive – it is the largest animal (that we know of) ever to have lived!

all about...

90

The percentage of a red panda's day that is spent in trees. They can be found in mountainous regions of China, Nepal and Myanmar.

35,000

The number of ants and termites consumed by a giant anteater every day!

50

A giraffe's tongue measures a lip-smacking length of 53 centimetres!

7

Despite having the longest neck of any animal, a giraffe has only seven bones in its neck – the same number as you!

ANIMALS

206

The number of Kakapo parrots left in the world. The kakapo is a flightless parrot that lives in New Zealand. There are so few of them that they all have been given individual names.

22

The number of hours a day a koala can spend sleeping!

237

Internet

in numbers

8
worldwide and **WONDERFUL** web-based stats...

1971
is when the first email was sent.

6/8/1991
The date when the FIRST WEBSITE was PUBLISHED. It is still live! Just go to info.cern.ch to CHECK IT OUT.

500 HOURS
of video are uploaded to YouTube every hour!

40,000

is the number of **GOOGLE SEARCHES** made every second.

That's around **3.5 BILLION** searches every day.

126 MILLION

people play the game Minecraft.

2.7 BILLION

The number of **MONTHLY USERS** of the social media website – FACEBOOK. It is the **BIGGEST SOCIAL MEDIA PLATFORM IN THE WORLD.**

989 MILLION

people use the internet in **CHINA.**

4.66 BILLION

The **number of people** who use the **internet today.**

That's well over **half the population** of the planet!

STAY **TUNED**

for music by numbers

4 The number of holes in the smallest playable harmonica.

1 The harmonica is the best-selling musical instrument worldwide!

10,000 The number of moving parts in a standard piano.

103 The longest piano concert ever played lasted for 103 hours and 8 seconds!

50,000

In 1995, a flute was discovered in Slovenia. It had been carved from the thigh bone of a bear and is believed to be at least 50,000 years old.

59

The minimum number of pieces of wood needed to build a violin.

1,128

The number of compositions by German composer Johann Sebastian Bach.

£9.8 million

The amount paid for a violin called the 'Lady Blunt' after one of its early owners.

1.136

The number of seconds heavy metal song 'You Suffer' lasts.

1

Rick Allen is the drummer of rock band Def Leppard. He has one arm!

99

The age of Captain Sir Tom Moore when he reached number one in the UK charts.

THE ZERO HERO

Imagine a world with NO ZERO!

Zero wasn't always with us. Try adding 9 and 1 together without it though! For thousands of years, humans used number systems that didn't feature a zero at all, so inventing it made maths a lot easier for all of us. So, when and where did it all begin?

The concept of using a 'something' to represent 'nothing' or a space was first developed by the Babylonian people, 4,000 years ago. The word 'zero' comes from the Arabic word 'sifr' which is a translation of the Sanskrit word 'sunya'. Indian mathematician Pingula referred to sunya over 2,000 years ago. Another Indian mathematician, Bhrahmagupta, was the first to describe the mathematical rules for zero in the 7th century. It would take another 500 years for zero to reach Europe!

Without the number zero, mathematics—and the world as we know it—wouldn't exist. For instance, without zero, calculus—the mathematic system for calculating rates of change—could not have been created. Calculus is used in physics and engineering and can tell us about things like the movements of the planets and stars, electricity and the weather. Without zero, the binary system (that only uses 0 and 1) wouldn't have been possible—and all modern computing is built on this system.

ZERO is a BIG DEAL

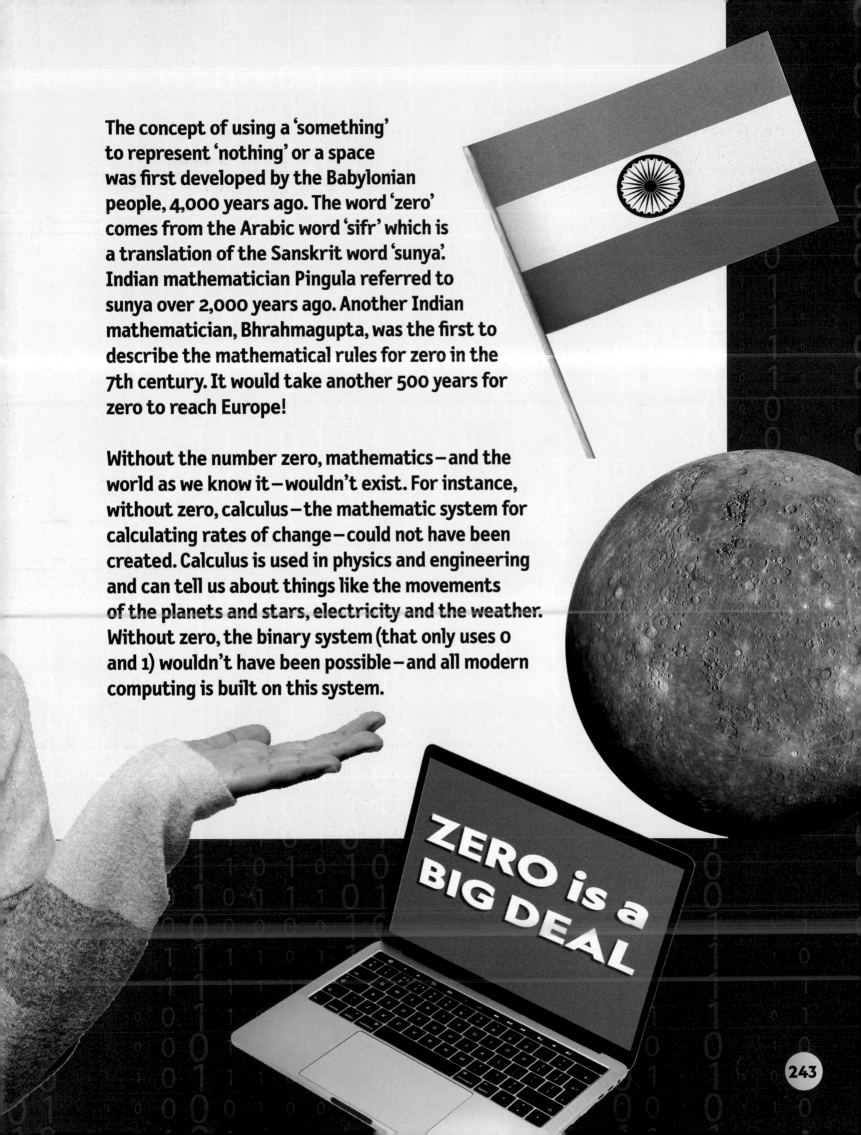

Index

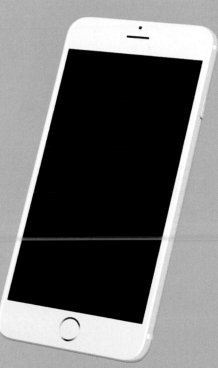

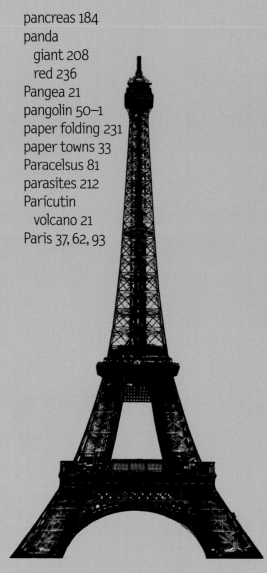

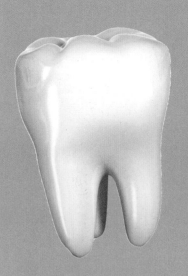

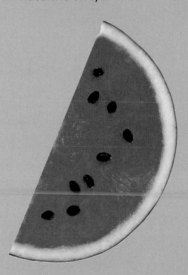

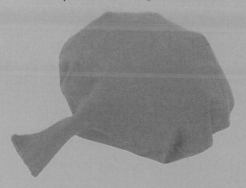

Image credits